A Year Amongst
The UK

Notes on Character and Culture in England
in 1973-1974

Arthur Asa Berger

A Year Amongst
The UK

Notes on Character and Culture in England
in 1973-1974

Illustrated by the Author

Marin Arts
PRESS

Contents

Preface

This book was written in 1973-1974, during a yearlong sabbatical in England. My family and I lived in London but I did a good deal of lecturing and managed to visit many other cities and universities during the year. I've also traveled a good deal in England and Scotland in 1958, before I got married.

It is an interpretation of English character and culture as I observed it during the year I was there. I never thought I'd be able to publish it because it was typed by one of our neighbors, who was a professional typist. I more or forgot about it, but one day while looking through my files I found it. Thanks to the magic of Optical Character Recognition I was able to turn the manuscript into a Word file and thanks to Word 2013 I was able to format it so I could publish it.

We must keep in mind that the book was written fifty years ago and does not describe contemporary England or London, now also known as Londonstan. It is also, you will discover, highly opinionated and probably full of absurd notions. That, it turns out, is the kind of books I write. Now, considering my interests, this book might best be described as an ethno-semiotic analysis. I've taken certain signifiers of English culture and character and tried to figure of what they signified.

I did the drawings in this book. Some of them come from a journal I kept during our year in London.

We got our house in London thanks to a friend, Pauline Todd, who I've known since 1958. She also was extremely kind to me and my family when we there and it is to her memory that this book is dedicated.

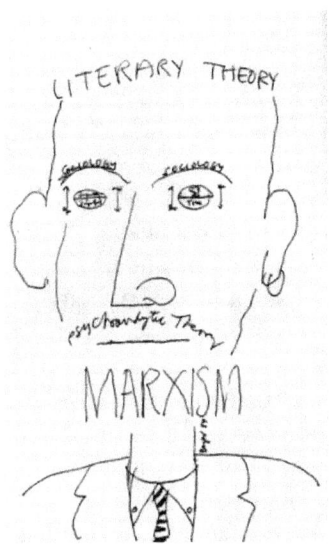

INTRODUCTION IN WHICH THE AUTHOR EXPLAINS HIS PURPOSES

This book is s rather perverse one (maybe even polymorphous, perverse). It is really a pop anthropological field study of English culture and, in particular, everyday life in London - though the format is often that of a travel story with opinionated "speculations" on this and that. I came to England to study the people there—much the same way an anthropologist might study savages inhabiting some remote island in the South Seas. After all, there is no reason why we must limit ourselves to head hunters in New Guinea or Brazil, or cave men in the Philippines.

The Englishman has a culture, too (though he is not, as a rule, a "cultured" individual), and his culture is susceptible to the some kind of analysis as is that of some non-literate tribe or primitive culture in the jungle. The title of this book, *The Uk,* is a play on a famous study of a tribe known as The Ik, who live in Uganda.

Thus I have been concerned with the general structure of English character and with such things as Wimpy burgers, milk (in bottles), advertisements, comics, sports and various other aspects of English everyday life. I am by profession a professor and my subject is popular culture--an umbrella term that covers a multitude of interests, and subjects. Most of my books have been held generally to be too deep for the ordinary man and not deep; enough for the scholar. Others have accused me of having too fertile an imagination, and one or two of insanity. I hope that you will have a better opinion of my efforts.

But I do think that imagination is important and, in a sense, I believe this book is as much a feat of imagination as anything else. This book carries on where I left off in a previously published effort, *The Evangelical Hamburger* (whose title essay is about the McDonald's hamburger chain as having the same dynamics as evangelical religions), except that this book is not just a series of essays but is, in part, a narrative of my adventures and a record of my opinions, observations and ideas about English (and in particular London) culture and character. It took a few weeks for us to get settled in a house I rented in Golders Green and then I went off to a conference in popular culture to start my year off on the right track.

A POP CULTURIST CONFERENCE: A TASTE OF ENGLISH ACADEMIC LIFE

It takes two hours by train to get to Norwich. I arrived at 3.30 with some other professors. We were met by people from the University of East Anglia, which was hosting the conference. We piled into a bus and were driven to the university, where we were each assigned rooms, given packets of materials, and meal tickets.

My room was a small one, with a small bed, a desk, two lamps, and a closet. The bed was over drawers; no space was wasted and nothing about the room was particularly lavish. But it did have a mattress, and across the hall was a big, beautiful bath. I was to spend a good deal of time in that bath, soaking and meditating.

I was to give a brief presentation on the comics at this conference and had sent 200 slides of various comics ahead, from San Francisco State College. They hadn't arrived! By this time I must admit I was not surprised; nothing in England seemed to work the way it should and I had almost come to expect that in any given situation, if something could go wrong, it would!

The University of East Anglia, in Norwich, can best be described as a modernist school, built after the second world war, which from certain points of view looks interesting; yet it has the ambiance of a prison. It is built of grey cinder blocks, is connected by aerial walkways (which are not covered so they don't protect people from rain) and is, for some reason, terribly oppressive. It has some vast green fields around it, but nobody seems to spend much time on them and they are uninteresting. In the center of the school is a shopping complex, with a small supermarket, a bookstore, some banks and that kind of thing. The dining hall is also located there.

The first day we had a reception hosted by the Lord Mayor of Norwich, who looked as if he had just stepped off the label of a Beefeater's Gin bottle. We formed in line, were announced by a lackey, and stepped up to shake hands with his eminence and a few other dignitaries. I was wearing a torn green sweater and some bush pants. He was not impressed!

At the reception a number of elderly ladies, all of whom seemed to tremble slightly, poured wine and served soggy canapés. But everyone was quite hungry and the food disappeared quite rapidly, as did the wine. We then went off to dinner at the school, in the faculty lounge, where a maître d' in tails and white gloves supervised a half dozen waitresses who served an elegant supper of trout and peas, and a lovely Charlotte Russe for dessert. The evening meals were all quite fancy and, for the most part, delicious.

The conference opened that night with a speech by Leslie Fiedler that was somewhat tangential to popular culture, but most of the pop culturists there were from English departments and they tended to see pop culture as popular literature along with a few other considerations. Benjamin DeMott was there, also, and a number of people from English Universities, who lectured on architecture, sociology and music, amongst other matters.

Everything was highly structured yet, curiously, leisurely. We broke for tea every morning and afternoon, had a reception every evening at 6.00 p.m. and had long dinners. Yet there was a lot going on and most of the people there attended a surprisingly high number of lectures and presentations. It may have been that we were isolated and there was little else to do? Norwich proper was about 15 minutes away by bus, and not too many people had the energy to go there. I met a number of interesting people and the conference was most useful in that regards. The French Cultural Attaché in London was there, and I discovered he was interested in the comics, so we had a good time talking about them; I also met Benjamin DeMott, whose work I've long admired, and a number of other intelligent and charming people. At the end we were all exhausted and wandered off in different directions. I had given my name and address to a dozen different people, and many of them had promised to get in touch or send me material I might use.

I rode back to London on the train with a woman named Clare who worked for Pan books ad was at the conference on a scouting mission, and Armand, a lawyer who represents a company that builds themed parks and is planning one for Paris. The stop before London a man and his wife entered our car, which was in second class but was only occupied by six people, informed me brusquely to move aside, and wedged himself in beside me. His wife did the same across from him. There was a

sense of rightfulness about the man that struck me as
typically English. The English, I believe, have a sense
of what is due to them, what is correct, and are insistent
on getting their due. I learned later that this called "right
mindedness." It had not occurred to this man and his
wife, I imagine, to look at any of the other cabins many
of which were half occupied. Our cabin was probably
nearest the place where he entered and he intruded into
the cabin, demanding his "rights." He tried to strike up a
conversation and informed me he was in "security" work.
When the train arrived at Liverpool Street Station, I said
to Armand "nous sommes arrive" – since he seemed to
prefer to speak in French. To my surprise, the man said
"That's not how it is pronounced, you know!" With that
he took his bags and left the car as abruptly as he had
entered it.

THE PAINTING PROFESSOR:
ORGIASTIC EXPERIENCES WITH EMULSION
AND THE ENGLISH SCHOOL SYSTEM

When I returned my family was at our friend Pauline's
house, so I had a sandwich and started making plans for
the next week. The big problem was getting a school for

our daughter Miriam. Our son Gabriel would go to the school in the neighborhood, but Miriam was eleven and finding a school that had room for her was to be a problem. However, our gas was connected - the man came the day I left for the conference, so that was one hurdle we had overcome. We also had received a note from a doctor who lived around the corner accepting us into his group practice, so that was taken care of and I was now in the National Health Service. And Bernie, our landlord, had bought some cheap paint for me, though it has been tinted cream and not "off-white" as I had asked. I used it in the hallway and it was okay.

My wife was frantic, though, over Miriam's school. She had called a number of places and didn't seem able to find anything. That morning she was just about to wander off to the phone booth when she thought, just for the hell of it, she'd try the phone. I picked it up and we heard a buzz. A great triumph. This meant we now had access to people. I went upstairs and called the school board, in order to see what I might be able to arrange. We figured that if we kept assaulting them, we might prevail. When someone from the school board answered the phone I said "This is professor Berger from the United States. I'm in London doing research and wonder whether you might be able to find a place for my daughter who is eleven." The woman paused for a moment to look through some files she had and then said, "Yes, we can take your daughter and told me the name of the school. So that matter was settled.

There was a different cast to everything in England; I could not help but marvel that though I was brought up in a society that was heavily influenced by English culture, English society was so strange to me in certain ways. I liked London and England, but I didn't think I'd ever want to live there permanently, for reasons which it is hard to put my finger on. England is very civilized and while London is not typical of England, it has a vitality and lusty quality that I find exhilarating.

And yet, there is some kind of a vague and diffuse unsettled feeling I get from living here. The reference points are not the same; the food tastes a bit different; the stores have strange brand names; the buses are fantastic and wonderful, when you can get on them. I actually registered at the police office a bit late, because I had done some touring and had been occupied with a million tasks, not the least of which was painting. I had to order coal. We had to get the telephone connected. We had to get a television set. We had to get utensils. We had to get a mattress (for myself), beds for my children, stationery, lamps, etc. And in each case there was usually some kind of a complication that made things difficult. Lamps, for example, are sold without plugs, since there are two different kinds of electrical systems in the homes here. These plugs are very fancy contraptions that have three prongs - one of which is for grounding things. I found myself at first at a loss when it came to doing something as simple as connecting the plugs to the lamp. I also had to have an electrician come in to connect some lamp, since I knew nothing about how the electricity worked.

We were in our house for three weeks before we had lighting in all the rooms; I called the electricity board to have a man come down, but they could only promise that he'd come s. particular day, without any indication as to when he would come. It was a minor inconvenience but an inconvenience nevertheless, for one of us had to wait around the house all day to make sure that someone would be home when he called around.

England is a country that might be characterized as having a number of minor inconveniences which are offset by the wonderfully humane and civilized nature of the life style led there. The English are not efficient, by American standards, but generally speaking they are much more kindly, more pleasant, more polite. After a while the general tone of civility becomes, infectious. I noticed that even my son Gabriel, a young savage, seemed to be much more polite and restrained.

Eventually, after making a number of phone calls and chasing about, we had achieved a measure of stability and had enough pots to cook in and enough plates to eat from and enough chairs to sit on; our children were properly uniformed and in school, and I had started investigating English culture and character. Actually, taking the house the way it was, was most useful in that it gave me a sense of what it is like to live in London the way Londoners do. I had to fight the various bureaucracies and establish myself, and get my family established. Fortunately I had brought a wad of travelers checks with me, which started disappearing at an alarming rate. The biggest drain on my pocket-book was my car which, it turned out, had defective brakes and needed a good deal of work - in addition to the muffler. The car cost £450 but by the time I had it fixed up, it ran me another $950, and became, in the final analysis, a rather costly "bargain." I had actually anticipated that the car would cost me some money to maintain, but not as much as it did.

The intriguing thing about getting settled in London was that no sooner did we take care of all the things we had to do on one list than other tasks presented themselves to us. The children needed felt-nib pens or baking pans for cooking class; we needed better knives - it was a constant stream of racing like crazy to keep up with the various obligations that kept pressing on us. I spent several weeks painting the walls of the house. The week that followed the "great painting orgy" was a mopping-up operation, in which I picked up s kitchen table for ten dollars at the local Oxfam. After we had stripped the linoleum off the dining room floor I called Oxfam and gave them the dining room rug, and the cushions that went underneath the rug, as well as a pair of Miriam's old shoes and a few other odd bits and pieces. The day after Oxfam came, I was walking by the place and decided to venture in - to see what they might have (Oxfam is a charity that operates s series of used furniture and household objects stores throughout London, much like the Salvation Army in America.) One of the volunteers there came up to me and said:

"We have a lovely rug that you might like." I smiled a bit.

"Come", she said, "I'll show it to you." She took me to the front of the store, where the rug I had given them the day before was displayed. I couldn't help but laugh. "1 gave you that rug yesterday", I said. Then she laughed. "Well", she added, "is there anything else you can use?

"A kitchen table," I said.
She then went to the counter area and had a short, whispered conversation with one of her colleagues.

"Well", she said, "we just got a kitchen table the other day. We didn't plan on selling it, since we wanted to display things on it, but you can have it for four pounds." She unloaded a number of things from a table that was hidden by a large, dirty tablecloth, and there was a table that was just perfect for our kitchen.

"How much did you say that was?" I asked, with a bit of a frown.

"Four pounds - but you can have it for three and a

half."

I paid her, grabbed the table and lugged it to our house, just a few blocks away, where I proceeded to paint it white. When the white dried I painted the top portion with yellow enamel. We were getting a lot of mileage out of our two cans of paint. In the back of my mind the idea of getting a third color started forming, but it lacked resolution and so did I.

Miriam and Gabriel made some lovely drawings with their felt nib pens and I stuck their drawings in a couple of frames that were lying about the house and put them up in the kitchen. It had become the nicest room in the house, and the one in which we would be spending a major portion of our time here.

TEL: 01-499 4316

Gentlemens' Hairdressing

ARTHUR BERGER
6 SHEPHERD STREET
SHEPHERD MARKET, MAYFAIR
LONDON, W1Y 7LN

ALIEN NOTIONS ABOUT AN ALIEN NATION: SPECULATIONS OF QUESTIONABLE VALIDITY UPON ENGLISH CULTURE AND CHARACTER

I had come to England to explore English culture and character. Well - I was getting some valuable insights of a kind not likely to be duplicated by the average

American. I had plugged into the society in the most literal sense of the term - at the household level. This meant I had to struggle with the British electrical system, which means that when you buy hairdryers or irons, you get them without plugs – since there are two different plugs (the round and the square) to fit into the two wiring systems (the old and the new) here. You must purchase plugs and put them on yourself.

This, however, is further complicated by the fact that some companies have changed colors for various wires, so that you frequently get plugs with one set of instructions, and appliances with another, and you must be careful that you put the correct wires into the correct sockets. The plugs frequently come with small fuses, which means that if there is a malfunction or overload, the plug "blows" and not the system itself. One day, I remember it well, my wife had rushed out to Woolworths to get a hairdryer and came dashing home so she could shampoo her hair and set it in time for a tea she was invited to that afternoon.

At least I got this without the usual fuss and inconvenience," she said, as she plunked the carton down. As she did, a monstrous thought crossed my mind and what I feared was soon to come true. She opened the box and pulled out the hairdryer. The wire attached to the hairdryer was coiled neatly, and at the end of this were three shiny pieces of wire and no plug. "Damn it", she cried, and I could understand how she felt. Since arriving in England we had felt a subtle and diffuse kind of resistance permeating the atmosphere. Somehow everything we tried to do was absurdly difficult. There was an element of culture shock about this - we were in an unfamiliar ambiance, though we spoke the same language and had many common traditions.

In England you had to grope, somehow, to do even the simplest things. If you didn't mind devoting your life to surviving - going shopping every day, washing clothes every day, doing things in bits and pieces without much concern for finalities, England posed few problems - you merely waited and did without, until, somehow, you found what you wanted or somebody did what you wanted them to do. I met people in England who spent ten years or more contemplating certain things that they thought they might like to do. I could well understand this, for the subtle pressure of English culture, which puts people in their place, which contains many privileges for some (and privilege means benefits for some at the expense of others) exudes a subtle kind of resistance to change; everything requires so much effort that after a while you succumb.

We had started our year in England with a visit to Battle Abbey and in some curious way that visit had given me a perspective on contemporary English culture. The styles have changed now. Instead of walking about in medieval garb or coats of armor, the modern Englishman wears a suit (and the younger Englishman sports flared and cuffed elephant pants, high-heeled platform shoes, etc.) but the impact of the medieval world is still powerful. For society now, as then, is divided up into two realms – the peasants and the lords, and that division has been and is all-important. There is, in England, a sizeable middle-class, but the important division is between the world-view and activities of the lords and the peasants or the commoners. Politically this division may not be too important, but psychologically and culturally it remains.

America, as Emerson described it, is a land without history; England is a land with too much, I would suggest. England is a medieval land that has been transmogrified into an almost modern one, but has notbeen able to escape its past. The following chart contrasts the two cultures most clearly.

ENGLAND	AMERICA
Medieval	Post-Modern
The Father	The Son
The Past	The Future
Once powerful, now weak	Once weak, now powerful
Sense of Place	Placelessness
Location	Rootless
Class bound	Mobile
Queue	Push ahead in lines
Small Island	Vast Continent
Cosmopolitan	Nationalist
Ascription	Achievement
Godless	Pious
Aggression turned inward	Aggression turned outward
Guilt	Murder
Architecture of Power	Architecture of Money:
Parliament, Castles	Skyscrapers
Specialists	Generalists

The key to the chart I've made up lies in the fact that, as see things, England is still medieval, in temperament and style, as well as other respects, though some of the nouveau riche in the business world can approximate the lordly life-style) live in the mansions and the peasants in the flats, and though the peasant may be mobile in many cases, their lives are "non-U" and petty.

The very architecture of England, its monumentality (especially London) and sense of tradition reinforces all that I've been talking about. I realize, of course, that London is not England, and that all generalizations (including this one) are suspect; but a visitor cannot help but be impressed by the pressure of place upon people. The politeness of the English is legendary, and is tied to this sense of place. The English "know their place," and if they forget, they are soon reminded of it. (Being a nation of fish eaters they also know their plaice.)

This politeness is, in part, a function of the pressure exuded by English culture on people not to show their feelings openly; not to exhibit in overt form, aggression. Thus, the English turn their aggression against themselves, which leads to a diffuse sense of guilt. This sense of guilt is reinforced by the State religion, which is now a hollow shell. England is a Godless and pagan nation. It was founded before Christianity and despite all the machinations of various God-fearing souls, the English have never been hesitant to bend religion to their will. Henry VIII knew what he was doing.

Modern London is certainly one of the pagan capitals of the world, and a pious and God-fearing country like America is so immensely more spiritual than England that it is even folly to compare the two countries in this respect. London, and perhaps England, has been recognized now by the Indian mystics as a missionary area for spiritualists and fakirs of every description: from Billy Graham in the West to fifteen year old "perfect masters" in the East. England may abound with Vicars and arch-bishops, but they are ornaments which sustain the illusion that a pagan land is a spiritual one.

Psychologists tell us that children usually inherit the super-ego of their parents. Thus America, the son, has been saddled with the super-ego (stemming from the immense piety that once characterized this land) of the fatherland, England. America, as Niebuhr once said (adapting the title of his book), is a pious and secular land; England, I would assert, is a pagan one and a Godless one.

Most Americans have the most absurd notions of what Englishmen are like; until fairly recently we only saw Oxbridge types--polished, aristocratic gentlemen who said "is-sue" instead of "ish-oo" (which is how Americans pronounce issue) and spoke beautifully. The rest of our American stereotype of the English and England was full of quaint villages and stately cathedrals and that kind of garbage.

Less than 5% of the people attend Church regularly. The fact of the matter is that England is a working-class nation. On the top of a veritable mountain of working-class souls exists a substantial layer of middle class types and a very thin layer of aristocrats and really privileged elites. But it is the working-class people who are the fiber that binds this land together and keep it going, and quite likely they are as abused now as they were a thousand years ago, when they were serfs or peasants. I have read Richard Hoggart's *The Uses of Literacy* and *Akenfield* and have in many respects a profound admiration for these people; my point is that the typical Englishman is not Anthony Eden or "Super Mac."

There is, of course, no such thing as an average Englishman or American, but it is possible to offer generalizations that seem to have a fair measure of

validity about national character and abstractions of that
sort. At this particular moment I don't know what the
national myth of England is. The American myth is what
is called "The American Dream," the notion that one can
create oneself, so to speak--that one can rise from humble
beginnings and, as Benjamin Franklin remarked in his
auto-biography, "sit with kings." This notion of the self-
made man stands at the core of the American psyche,
though this dream is beginning to fade and Americans are
becoming less intoxicated by illusion. The American
Dream is that of protean man, of man without a past and
history and tradition to hold him down. The future is
everything for the American.

For the Englishman it is the past that is glorious. England
is now a third-rate power in the world; it may be a great
moral force (it certainly seems to think it is) but it does
not have many more divisions than the Pope. When I was
growing up in Boston, in the fourth or fifth grade, we had
a map of the world on the wall in which each country
was given a color. England was pink (how appropriate),
and a great deal of the world was colored pink at that
time - India, Canada, large parts of Africa, Australia,
and on and on. We all learned about the sun never setting
on the British Empire.

It did not take long, however, for that vision to vanish,
leaving a conglomerate of autonomous and semi-
autonomous nations with complicated relationships to the
United Kingdom. And as that empire vanished so did
England's power. Thus the English are left with
remembrances of empires past and with a "glorious"
history. I must confess that when I took an advanced
course in English History during my undergraduate days
I found it terribly boring. This may have been the fault of
my instructor who seemed to have an uncanny capacity

to force my eyes to close shortly after he started opening his mouth. I slept through the War of the Roses, Long and Short Parliaments, the succession of innumerable houses to the throne, anda mountain of details that seemed to be of no real import.

And I must confess that I find it almost incomprehensible to think that this nation of slightly post medieval (for England is still medieval), inefficient, bumbling clowns was the greatest power in the world for a positively ridiculous length of time. The English are charming, highly intelligent, frequently eccentric, kindly and generally delightful on a person-to-person basis, especially if you are mixing with the educated and cultured elite. Still, they exploited a good deal of the world for hundreds of years; they brought Christianity and took raw materials.

For the average man-in-the-street, the descendant of the peasant or serf, security is basic and tied to that security are various rights that must be respected. There is little adventure for the common man – other than vicarious excitement from football and rugby, wrestling, and various other sports. Perhaps the English even find cricket exciting; from what I've seen of it, it is a terribly monotonous game which takes forever and lacks pressure and dynamism. I do not understand the finer points of the game, but what I've seen on television has not kindled a fondness for the sport. The only real action and adventure for the working man is "going out;" that is, the strike! "Going out" is a subject that seems to mean a great deal to the Englishman; you find it popping up in his humor all the time. It is an overt act, in a sense, but it is also passive - it involves a refusal to perform customary activities, a kind of withdrawal. I suspect that "going out" has immense psychic gratifications for the working classes; when they go on strike they are broadcasting, to the elites who survive off their labors, that they recognize the situation and are willing to paralyze society if they are not treated slightly better.

It is a modern variation of the great (and frequently violent) strikes that took place in late medieval Europe, when weavers and other workers also "went out" (though during these days the workers were generally brutally beaten down). "Going out", then, is the moral equivalent of war for the modern Briton, except that he battles multi-national corporations and industrial giants now, and not dragons and monsters. For the average working-class youth in a society in which advancement is based upon ascription (who you know, which in large part determines what you will know, or be able to know), the two paths that lead to fame and fortune are becoming a soccer star or a rock star. For the rest, except for a few bright boys who somehow make it to and through the university, there are plenty of jobs at 30 or 40 pounds a week (which is, so I've been told, the national average).

The rocker-soccer stars are national heroes who symbolize, in a certain sense, the hopelessness in which their followers find themselves. England is a humane country and its lords still have remnants of a sense of social obligation and noblesse oblige. In 1776 Adam Smith developed the notion of laissez-faire which, in effect, freed bourgeois manufacturers and businessmen from the restrictions that had characterized relations between the landed gentry (the feudal lords) and the peasants. The "market" was to take care of all problems, and if there were problems in an economy it was because, so Adam Smith explained, government interference was preventing the "invisible hand" (which transformed the selfishness of each into the welfare of all) from working properly. This crass and absurd doctrine was very popular in England and, to a certain extent, is popular now in America. But it never triumphed completely and the old medieval sense of obligation in the nobility (aided by pressure from the peasants, now organized into trade unions) has led to the development of a social-welfare service state.

I must say that I find it quite touching when I watch soccer on the television; the excitement of the fans, the chanting they do, the whole ambiance of the match - you gain a sense of community (or the possibility thereof} but the passion is all wasted on nonsense. The English are not quite as insane as Latin Americans about the game, but they do follow it closely and lionize its stars. It may be possible to make an equation in which there would be a direct relationship between the passion of the populace for soccer and singers and the general state of degradation in which the masses find themselves.

Thus the hooliganism which now seems to take place after matches has a social and a political dimension. It suggests that soccer no longer has the capacity to provide the release it hag for everyone, and that certain segments of the population now are resorting to violence and other kinds of "anti-social" behavior. The aggression which these young hooligans express in their violence marks a turning point in the English psyche. These young Englishmen no longer find relief for their aggression in vicarious thrills (soccer) or self-flagellation (guilt) but now express their aggression and anger directly and overtly, and against other people and society at large.

For the average Englishman, I suspect, life involves being part of a vast, undifferentiated blob of humanity, with no notice being taken of one's existence except for fellow workers, immediate neighbors and one's family - and a legion of hidden bureaucrats somewhere. Out of this mass of people emerge the rocker and soccer stars, various entertainers and other celebrities whose lives are "world-historical" and whose exploits are followed avidly. When there is little social mobility there is hardly a chance for most people to rise and be admired, and so they "live" vicariously through their heroes. .

What is strange to me, and this may be a function of my having been raised an American, is that these people seem to be regarded as legitimately remarkable people to whom admiration--and perhaps even honor--is due. In America the businessman is the hero and entertainers have a dubious and ambiguous status. All of this may be connected to class levels; it is quite possible that in both America and England, lower class and working class people share a passion for bread (in England it would be beer) and circuses, and the dream of becoming a star. It is star or nothing, and in most cases it is nothing. Thus you find that the faces of the typical Englishmen reflect a certain stoic sense of resignation, and, ultimately, of despair. Every Englishman is raised with a sense of his limitations, and while this gives him a certain kind of security (within the confines of his station), it also creates a kind of fatalism and passivity that is sad to behold. I feel a certain tiredness about the people here-- at least the older ones. Some of the younger ones - the students - are lively and have a sense of possibility, but students are a privileged minority in England. Less than ten percent of young people between 18 and 22 are in universities, and it was something like five percent just a half dozen years ago. For many young people in England it is out to work, at 15 - an age when the average youth in America can look forward to between three and six years more of education.

In California, for instance, about fifty percent of young people between 18 and 22 are in community colleges, state universities or the universities. (We have a three tiered system which is designed to take everyone who wishes higher education someplace. Everyone 18 or over can attend the community colleges for free, regardless of whether he has graduated from high school. After two years in the community colleges, he can transfer to the other schools for his last two years, leading to the B.A. or B.S. degree.)

Faces in America tend to reflect a mad lust for consumer objects. America, land of the future, is full of people who seem to have no object in life other than making and spending money. The vast and ubiquitous (and enormously powerful) advertising industry in America has created a nation of lustful souls, who ravage the environment and earth in a quest for bigger and more costly "toys." This lust is not for things in themselves but for things which will help them lead "the good life." Americans, it has been said, are "idealists" who work with matter, not materialists.

In contrast to the British sense of place, which leads to a reverence for the earth and a rather guarded approach towards things, the Americans have no sense of limit. Until the recent ecology movement Americans wasted their continent with nary a thought. (We still do - but now we worry about it.) The enormous size of the country and its vast wealth bred a sense of infinitude; there would be no end to anything, so everything could be grabbed, used and discarded, with hardly a thought about the consequences of this kind of action.

Thus the Americans wasted their possibilities prodigiously. America's vast wealth has been funneled into the consumer sector (television sets, cars, gadgets) while the public sector has been undernourished. Americans have yet to accept the reality of the welfare state, though they have the substance of it in many respects. (item: one out of every seven persons in New York City is on welfare.) Here in England I have a friend who is s doctor, a dentist and qualified psychiatrist. The country seems to have a small minority of extremely well educated people and a mass of poorly educated ones. The English educational system is, I've heard, admirably suited for the development of geniuses.

And so there are many people with hardly any education or money and a few with too much. After all, by the time he has reached eleven (and generally well before this age) the average person in England has a pretty distinct sense of his possibilities; if he cannot be a rocker or soccer star, he will be a milkman. At fifteen you can be making fourteen pounds a week in the post office - and, as their recruiting posters say, "that's only a start."

No wonder British faces reflect a sense of despair. At eleven they know they have no future, or, for the favored few, a life of privilege. (There is little room at the top and lots of room at the bottom.) The stores all have signs for clerks; living in England food is expensive but life is cheap.

In America at eleven children are just beginning to have dreams of glory and entertain the most fantastic illusions about their futures. They all expect to be bank presidents and doctors and lawyers and baseball players, and though many of them will find that their expectations are or were absurd, they pursue their dreams with an activism and energy that is startling. The American's sense of despair when he does fail (which may mean not realizing his fantastic expectations, but still doing pretty well) is bitter and personal.

The Englishman has no hopes and few expectations once his future has been determined at eleven or so. Thus he does not suffer the bitter sense of failure, of personal failure, which the American feels. The American has been led to believe that his future is in his own hands and that accidents of birth (the class he is born into) are inconsequential. The Englishman knows the score early; after all, every time he opens his mouth his accent betrays him. Thus the Englishman suffers from a lingering sense of despair; his options are few and he'd better make peace with himself. Malt does more than Milton can in this regards.

"Is it better to have loved and lost or to have never loved at all?" We may ask the same question about the sense of possibility. Is it better to dream and have that dream smashed or to never dream at all? I personally favor dreaming, because sometimes the dream sustains one and people do make their dreams come true, somehow. It is hard to conceive of people with no dreams at all--of people resigning themselves, at 15, to fourteen pounds a week.

THE SECRET AGENT REVEALS HIMSELF:
HE SEEKS THE FIGURE IN THE CARPET AND THE
MEANING OF SIGNIFICANT TRIVIA

How ironic. After having spent a summer painting and
fixing up my home in America (so I could rent it), I came
to London and found I had to spend some more time
painting and fixing up the house I was letting in London.
But after several weeks I finished most of my work
and began to pursue my research. I wrote several dozen
letters and made a number of 'phone calls and gradually
things began to materialize. I got a letter from Lucca 9
(The International Festival on the Comics) inviting me to
participate in a roundtable on Parapsychology and The
Superman, which I accepted. I had been anxious to go to
that conference since it began, and now, unless
something surprising happened, I would. The timing was
perfect--my book, *The Comic-Stripped American,* was to
appear the day after the conference got under way. A
remarkable coincidence.

I called someone at the Independent Broadcasting
Authority but he was in Scotland; however, I managed to
get my name on their mailing list, so I could get a feel for

what they were up to through their publicity. I called a
fellow at the British Broadcasting Corporation but he was
out to lunch--at 2.30, which struck me as strange, but
even more remarkably he returned my call and we made
an appointment to get together and talk.

Then I had received a letter and a copy of the *Public Arts
Review* enclosed in it, from my friend at Cambridge, a
senior tutor at one of the colleges there. So there was a
bit of action, at last. I had also written to the Centre for
Contemporary Culture at the University of Birmingham
and arrangements were being made for a visit there.
While all of this was going on I found myself dwelling
upon a number of different aspects of English life.
Certain key artifacts and practices were beginning to
suggest themselves to me and I was anxious to do some
work on them. I knew I would have to do something on
beer. It was central. Also Wimpy burgers. Cricket
seemed important, though I found it hard to get involved.

I had heard from many people that nobody pays
parking tickets in London, and I wanted to find out about
that. The institution of "booking" (and queuing which is
related to it) intrigued me, as did all the articles one could
buy marked "By Appointment to Her Majesty." There
were many other items that immediately attracted my
attention: things proudly labelled "British made," the
saying the "Best of British Luck to You," the British
Press, wrestling on the telly, Billy Butlin's holiday
camps, pubs and clubs, and so forth. To the Englishman
all of the things I've mentioned are taken for granted, part
of the natural stream of things. And none of these things
seem particularly important or worth bothering about.
And yet, there is some kind of a system of values and
beliefs that ties people together in this country and in
every country. There are certain key assumptions that

people hold here, and certain significant artifacts and
institutions that reflect these assumptions and reinforce
them, though in certain cases these institutions may also
be changing them.

What we are involved with, really; is a spy story. I am a
secret agent who came to London to find the national
secrets, to discern the hidden beliefs and assumptions of
the people there. My problem was made difficult by the
fact that what I was looking for was not isolated in some
safe, hidden away somewhere, but was all about me,
confusing me by its all-pervasiveness. What do you grasp
onto when you are trying to explain trendy people? They
are in miniskirts and platform heels one moment, but
when the current moves, are in something else. In any
case, I was out to "crack" the cultural code by explicating
the hidden significance of commonplaces.

What I was looking for use all about me, but because it
was so obvious I could not see it. It was only after I had
found the figure or pattern in the carpet that I was able to
snap my fingers and say "of course," but why didn't I see
it earlier, since it was so apparent? Things which seem
trivial and inconsequential take on significance once they
are put into perspective and worked into some kind of a
structure of meaning. I am interested in insights into
British culture? And what is an insight but the
recognition of meaning and relationship that one was
previously unaware of. Or at least one that you did not
realize you were aware of. After someone has pointed
out something to you and given you an insight, you often
have the feeling that you knew it all the time but never
brought it to the level of consciousness, for some reason.
And it is because so much of what I'm looking for is
pushed into the "cultural unconscious" of the English that
I really cannot ask them for what I seek. In a sense it is

helpful being an American, because I do not operate with the basic assumptions and frame of reference of the typical Englishman. I'm not used to cars approaching me from the right and, as a result, I've almost been hit a few times. I'm not used to being hounded by clerks when I enter a store; that is, I feel I'm being hounded because I'm not used to having such attention paid to me in stores. I'm not used to milk in bottles, especially pint ones (in America we usually purchase milk in half-gallon cardboard containers, though gallon containers are becoming popular now) nor am I used to the politeness of people here (except when they are driving cars, in which case they are absolutely terrible).

Like any spy I'm looking for signs and signifiers that will lead to the secrets I seek; there are little clues that are significant in that they point to more important ones and, ultimately, to insights and "secrets." These clues may be as trivial as the look on the face of a woman who has just lost at a "chicken tombola," or the behavior of a dozen motorists trying to negotiate a crossing, and each unwilling to give way to the other so that all are stuck. For me these things have resonance--they are indicators of people's view of things, hopes and expectations. For a case study let us look at the English driver.

THE ENGLISH DRIVER:
SET HIM ON A HORSE
AND HE WILL RIDE A GALLOP

I have always been astonished at the way people in England respond when I tell them that I find English drivers terrible. In England it is the Italians, French and Israelis who have a reputation for recklessness and perhaps even suicidal behavior on the road. The English think of themselves as rational, law-abiding, and courteous drivers. When I find fault with English drivers it has nothing to do with their driving ability or recklessness. What bothers me, aside from the speed with which traffic moves (when it can) on these narrow streets, is the attitude drivers in England toward pedestrians. I always feel that my life is in danger when I try to cross the street in England, even when I'm on crosswalks. And I must admit I have had several narrow escapes, caused by drivers who didn't seem to have the slightest concern for my well-being.

I may he spoiled because I come from California, where cars must give pedestrians the right of way at all times. Here the situation seems reversed; the pedestrian has to be careful and his rights are honored (whatever they may be) more in the breach than the practice. The way the English drive relates, I believe, to the prince-peasant structure of English society. In America we tend to think of the British as plodders. One element in the cultural stereotype is the people, and life moves slowly in England - and it may be so in most areas of life, but such is not the case for those wishing to catch buses. There is a curious situation--one never seems to arrive at a bus stop at the same time the desired bus arrives. You often find yourself about a block from a bus stop when a red bus looms in the distance and you have to run like crazy to get to the bus stop (frequently to find that the conductor won't let you on) or you arrive at a bus stop and wait in a queue that is enormous for a bus that never seems to come. I have been struck by the number of people I see running for buses, though that is probably common to all large cities. London is a very cosmopolitan city. The diversity shows in the restaurants, stores, newspapers, and colors of the skin of people walking (or running after buses) down the street.

I see the English driver as a carry-over of the mentality manifested in earlier times, when carriages raced along roads and through streets with little concern about whether people (peasants) were in the way, were run over, or trampled. The modern Briton is, when in his car, especially if it is a big one--in a situation where he has power and the command imperatives in his psyche are let loose. Driving seems to unleash all the worst in people, in all cultures but the way people respond when at the wheel probably differs a good deal from country to country. And it certainly must reflect certain culturally idiosyncratic and distinctive tendencies within a given society.

Thus the English, who are generally polite and "proper" on a face-to-face level are terribly aggressive and nasty when they can escape from outside pressures and unleash their true "selves." Motorized speed is one of the few channels available to the ordinary person in which he can, for a moment, give his power imperatives free (or moderately free) rein. It is because the English cannot control themselves when they break loose from their inhibitions that they kill themselves at such an alarming rate on some of the superhighways they build. At least that used to be the case if I recall some articles I've read on the subject. As an American who drives, when absolutely necessary (and even then with my heart in my mouth) in London, I must say I find it terrifying. But trying to cross the street is just as bad. In part it is because I'm never able to be secure or certain that somebody will not decide I'm a peasant--one of an undifferentiated mass of souls of no consequence, and run over me in his mad haste to get someplace of relative unimportance.

Volume XXVIII

(K) or The Constant ...
oct. 10, 1973

K
28

Arthur Asa Berger
9 Dingwall Gardens
LONDON N.W. 11
ENGLAND
Tel: 01-458-2638

AAB IN THE BBC:
SCOTCH EGGS AND SPECULATIONS
ON NOSTALGIA

I called a fellow I had contacted by mail at the BBC, and
was invited to Bush House to meet him and some of his
staff. I arrived at noon, on the dot, and went to a desk
where visitors register and wait to be escorted to
wherever they are going. I was brought to the seventh
floor of Bush house, which is relatively dingy, and
ushered into L's office, where I sat around and chatted
about my adventures here in London, popular culture,
etc. After a couple of strong gin and tonics we all
retreated to the BBC canteen, where we spent a couple of
more hours standing about and discussing politics,
education, life in America, the difference between
Oxford University and Cambridge University, why a
"second" was better than a "first" at such places, and a
number of other topics. It was very pleasant and after a

couple of pints of bitter (which is more than I usually have) I staggered off into London and everyone else staggered off to their respective offices. It was 3.45.

My host had purchased a plate of sandwiches, the classic English horrors which seem to be everywhere: white bread with the crust sliced off, filled with tomatoes or sardines or eggs. These sandwiches always, for some reason, seem slightly soggy, slightly moldy, and rather tasteless. You can eat them but you don't get much of a kick out of it. At least, hopefully, they provide nourishment?

One of his colleagues introduced me to something called a Scotch Egg--which I would describe as a hard-boiled egg surrounded by cement. The Scotch Egg has the capacity to stretch the stomach like nothing else I know of. It plummets down the furthermost recesses of the stomach, and then drags the stomach down to about your knee-caps by the force of its density Black holes and Scottish eggs are probably the two most dense entities in the universe. Perhaps not all Scotch Eggs are like that. The idea is a good one. You wrap an egg in sausage meat and cook it, so that you have sausages and eggs together in an easy-to-handle form. But the cooks at the BBC seem to have a genius for soggy sandwiches and impenetrable Scotch Eggs.

After you have enough of that good, strong English beer you forget about Scotch eggs and cucumber sandwiches, fortunately. And we had a pleasant and animated time of it. we had made arrangements for me to appear on a program, Open Door, and two days after my first visit to the BBC I was back, to record this program with a young fellow, Andrew W., who writes on contemporary culture for some English journals. We spent a half hour chatting, recorded a rambling and diffuse discussion (to put it most charitably) about revivals in America and England, and that was that.

Actually, the subject of revivals and nostalgia, and the curious fact that London is full of plays and shops that remind one (or were written) in the Thirties is something worth thinking about? But why people are nostalgic and why there should, theoretically by chance, be a lot of nostalgia for the thirties, and in particular the American thirties, is hard to fathom. Revivals always involve popular culture, for it dies quickly (generally speaking) in order that it can be discovered again. The classics are not really revived, in the sense that they are (supposedly) always alive; they have eternal value and universal truth, and as such, never lose their validity. We don't feel nostalgia about Shakespeare or Dante or Beethoven. But we do feel nostalgia for pop songs of ten years ago and things we ate when we were children. We wish to return to the past, but it is a romanticized and idealized past. I can remember recently I was invited to dinner at the home of an old family friend for whom I sheltered fond memories. I remembered her as being a "marvelous" cook, though I hadn't eaten at her house for many years. The meal we had was bland and tasteless. Even the dessert was poor. For years I had had marvelous memories (illusions) about the superb meals she made when I was a child. As an adult I discovered that my remembrances were all wrong.

On the cultural level the same process is at work. People yearn for simplicity and the good things they associate with their childhood and the good "old" days. Modern society is full of threats and anguish, as is adulthood, and so nations as well as individuals (or, at least, cities like London) frequently return, one way or another, to the imagined serenity of the old days. We associate absolute love with childhood; by that I mean that young children are not loved "conditionally" (the love being based upon the successful completion of tasks, the satisfaction of certain conditions) but without regard for performance.

Later on, love is given out or taken away on condition; we learn we have to earn love as well as our daily bread. The psychic cost of this process is devastating. Thus if it is possible to "return" to days when things were simpler and we did not have a "performance problem," we seize upon the opportunity gladly. Now this does not apply to young people today, since they are born under the threat of the atom bomb and cannot return to simplicity, except in terms of their imagination. For them, and for many others, the sheer novelty of change is persuasive. Change, the search for kicks, either in nostalgia or futurism, is what is important and it doesn't make too much difference which way the change leads them. It is the movement that they find so intoxicating.

There is another matter which must be mentioned here, which involves a sense of superiority we feel when we return to old, long-forgotten entertainments we once loved and realize that they are childish and absurd, and recognize this. We return, via revivals and nostalgia crazes, to the past, but only for a while and on our terms.

There is some kind of an intoxication with power and the capacity to throw oneself backwards and forwards through time that is at play.

Now why a particular period of time catches on is another matter, only partially explained by what I've said. For example, in London during the Fall of 1973, there are any number of plays and films from the American thirties, and even clothes have a thirties look about them. How does one explain this? I would guess that it is a combination of chance and the tendency of the media and entertainment worlds to imitate successes that has led to this blossoming of the American thirties in London. In addition, there just happened to be some pretty good things to revive.

ANGLO-SAXON ATTITUDES AND PLATITUDES

I went to the Gallup Poll people and spent an afternoon examining their files - that is, the ones they would let me see. I managed to find some interesting information about British attitudes and values which provides a pretty accurate picture of life in Britain. I discovered that only 35 percent of the women know how much money their husbands make, which seems incredible. A poll in February, 1973, discovered that the British are fairly satisfied with life in general, which is even more incredible. Below I offer some statistics about British public opinion and attitudes about a variety of topics.

SATISFIED WITH PERCENTAGES:

Housing	71%
Family income	49%
Work 7	1%
Leisure (amount of)	71%
Standard of living	74%
Honesty and standard of behavior of people	29%

These figures are striking to me, since I can recall seeing a poll in America which showed that most of the people there were far from satisfied.. The headline of the write-up of this poll went something like "Most Americans Leading Lives of Quiet Desperation!"

February 1974 found things considerably different in Britain and it is likely that these optimistic figures would not be duplicated. To find even half the English people content with their income is remarkable. Americans are brought up so that they are never content with their incomes, no matter how high. (There is always room for improvement in the American perspective.)

I find some British beliefs amusing, though it may be that Americans are equally as silly. Thus 18% of the population believes in the devil here. Some 30% "believe in" striptease shows, 41% in self-denial and 49% in chastity! Other beliefs or things that British people favor or that they don't favor follow:

TOPIC   FAVOR DON'T FAVOR

Death penalty	66%	44%
Evolution	32%	68%
School Uniforms	59%	41%
Patriotism	68%	32%
Modern Art	49%	51%
Strict Rules	46%	54%
Sunday Observance	44%	56%
Inborn Conscience	56%	44%
Bible Truth	56%	44%
Beatniks and Hippies	18%	82%
Royalty	75%	25%
Mixed Marriage	42%	58%

There are few correlations to be found here. The only items favored by 30 to 40% of the people are evolution, striptease shows and modern art, which may mean that people who believe in evolution like to see nude women, especially when they are descending staircases. At the top end of the scale there is a closeness between favoring royalty, being patriotic, and believing in the death penalty. History seems to bear out the fact that there is a strong connection between royalty, patriotism and death—especially for foot soldiers, so the linkage is both logical and historical. In August of 1973 a Gallup poll showed that the British are, as a rule, also satisfied with their basic institutions, as is shown below

TOPIC	GOOD VALUE	POOR VALUE
Police	79%	16%
National Health Hospitals	78%	17%
General Practitioners	74%	24%
Universities	62%	13%
Secondary Schools	60%	19%
Garbage Collectors	67%	29%
Employment Benefits	50%	21%
Pensions, Retirements	28%	61%

These figures are also startling. They indicate that the British feel much more positively about the police and their educational system than Americans do. In fact a 1969 poll shows that 35% of the British said that they see themselves as "very happy" and that 55% see themselves as happy. That is 90% of the people are happy or very happy! This also contrasts with America where a sizeable number of people do not consider themselves happy and are dissatisfied with their jobs, wives, cars and local football teams.

The reason why the British are happy (or think they are happy, or claim to be) and the Americans are unhappy is that there is an inverse correlation in America between what people expect and what they get. To put it in dramatic terms, Americans think they all should be kings and are unhappy even if they are nobles, and Englishmen generally think of themselves as peasants, and are grateful for any favors (and motor cars) big and small. The National Health Service (both hospitals and doctors) are considered to be "good value" and have great support. This poll, conducted in August of 1973, suggests that large numbers of Americans have a distorted view of the way the English feel about their Health Service. In America there seems to be a general belief (thanks to the AMA, no doubt) that the National Health Service has been a "disaster", and that American entrepreneurial medicine is the proper structure for medicine, in that it is founded on greed, the only incentive we believe for "efficiency".

There is one aspect of life here that I find quite intriguing. Almost everyone I have met has something nasty to say about garbage collectors or "dustmen," as they are called in Britain. They are all villains, if you listen to your neighbors, who spend half their time out on strike, and who have to be given extra money if anything the least bit extraordinary is desired. Yet 67% of the people think they are getting good value from them What this demonstrates is that there is a marked tendency in the Englishman and Englishwoman to grumble about trivial things, perhaps only to hear oneself talk, if nothing else. The average Englishman's passion is reserved for soccer and politics since, by definition, Englishmen may not take an active interest in sex. (One of the popular plays in London is called "No Sex Please, We're British.") The so-called sexlessness of the British is a national joke and the British revel in the stereotype of themselves as sexless and cold. Actually, breast fetishism here is a national obsession as reflected in the popular press.

What has happened is that the "sexless, lifeless, inhibited" stereotype of certain upper-class types has been applied by foreigners to the British in general. There is probably an element of truth in the stereotype. The upper-class British sense of humor relies on understatement and a kind of passionless, bloodless equanimity. This reserve and quiet rectitude are part of upper-class manners and the upper-class heritage. (This type of personality structure may be closely connected with the desire to maintain social distance; it is not a national characteristic by any means.) In fact, the British see themselves as friendly. In a September 1973 Gallup poll on stereotypes, the British compared themselves with Americans in a number of different aspects:

	U.5.A.	ENGLAND
Friendly	35%	43%
Efficient	27%	17%
Intelligent	19%	22%
Hard working	16%	25%
Insincere	15%	6%
Intolerant	9%	6%
Humorless	7%	5%

Poor	2%	6%

These figures were elicited from a question that asked "which adjectives best describe the people of?" and offer a vague kind of self-portrait of the English. It is obvious that the English feel themselves generally superior, even if poorer, than Americans.

For example, they consider themselves to be friendlier, more intelligent. English people consider themselves to have these characteristics in greater numbers than they believe them to exist in America. The only area where the English feel Americans are superior is in efficiency (and perhaps its logical extension, wealth). Nevertheless, the English (despite their inefficiency) have great hopes for "pie in the sky" when they die.

In May of 1973, 51% of the English believed in heaven and 74% believed in God; this despite the fact that 70% of them feel that religion is losing its influence on British life. The British see "class struggle" as an important feature of life--57% believe that there is class struggle as contrasted with 29% who don't see it as important. Ten percent of the British have been robbed and they believe it takes £10.56 (approximately $26.50) a week to feed a family of four. The average salary here is less than £40 ($100) a week.

The British believe that the most influential groups and personages are: the Prime Minister (75%), Big Business (68%), Trade Unions (73%), the Royal Family (14%) and the Church (17%). The royal family is popular but the average Englishman does not think it is very influential. There is always a danger, of course, of reading too much into statistics and it is frequently an error to assume that people actually believe what they say they believe or will do what they think they are going to (or would like to) do. I purchased some junk furniture while in London and the last time I was in the store I trade at I happened to get into a conversation with a salesman there. It turns out he had read great amounts of Emerson, Thoreau, Dreiser, Sinclair Lewis, Mark Twain and a number of other writers, and everything by Jack London and a good deal about him.

Where would this man fit in the statistical profile I've been sketching? The British sociologists divide the country up into six classes: A, B, C1, C2, and E., much the same way we divide American society into six classes: upper-upper, lower-upper, upper-middle, lower-middle, upper-lower and lower-lower. But would one imagine that a salesman in a used-furniture store would have such a remarkable familiarity with American literature? "I used to read a lot when I was younger," he told me. He mentioned also that heliked Upton Sinclair and Bret Harte.

Statistics and opinion-sampling really don't take this kind of person into account; people measure what they can, and I suppose we must be grateful for whatever we can get from these people. They have not had remarkable success in predicting--or is it forecasting--election results but probably are quite accurate about what they measure, especially when they are concerned with specific issues. There is, of course, a statistically "typical" Englishman, and he has been described in the September 27th issue of *Radio Times* (page 16):

Mr. and Mrs Average had:

two children (34.9 per cent of married couples have two children)
a semi-detached house (33 per cent of homes) which isn't theirs'
(49.7 per cent of small families have a mortgage)

a fridge (69 percent of homes)
a washing-machine (64 per cent)
a television (91 per cent)
a telephone (maybe - 38 per cent)
a car (44 per cent)

Mr. Average has
a life expectancy of 68.06 years
a job as a skilled manual worker (40.6 per cent of employees)
a pay packet oi' £38.48 per week

Mrs. Average has
a life expectancy of 74.9 years
plans for starting work when the kids are off her hands
(42.8 per cent of mothers say this)

The Children have
education up to age l6 (64.4 per cent in 1971)
a job as soon as they leave school (77 per cent)

This portrait shows a reasonable level of well-being, though by American standards the average Englishman (and family) are, at best, only moderately comfortable. When I was in the Army I had a "buddy" (as friends in the Army are called) who was a convinced Anglophile. He dreamed of fancy tweeds and aristocratic clerks in bowlers (derbies). After his first trip to London he returned, his dreams in shreds, for he had found that England is a working class society, and the average Englishman has little money, poor taste and not much elite "culture." That is, the average Englishman is not that much different from the average person from any place in the western world.

Americans harbor fantasies about what might be called the Cosmopolitans," the European man who has "class," is cultured, has a way with the ladies, has perfect manners, and knows how to "live," whatever that might mean. But most Englishmen have not gone to Oxford or

Cambridge; the average Englishman is a skilled laborer who reads the *Mirror* or some other scandal sheet and is as far-removed from being a cosmopolitan as is a bootblack in Los Angeles. This does not mean that London and England are not delightful places to visit and that the countryside is not beautiful, the people friendly and charming, London exciting, and so forth. It is merely that the English are not what we think they are. I would also argue that they are not what they think they are. (The Cockney-eyed view we have of the English is, in great part, the result of mass media stereotyping.)

WRESTLING ON THE TELLY

I have always been interested in watching wrestling on television; I don't mean the sport as practiced by college students but the exhibition as practiced by a legion of actor-athletes who seem to be everywhere you go, grunting and groaning, throwing their opponents out of the ring, and carrying on in certain ways to which we have more or less become accustomed. Because I believe that we "learn" from our experiences, I have argued (in an essay called "The Politics of Wrestling") that the wrestling we see on television reinforces certain values and provides certain models for imitation.

That is, wrestling has a point of view--it posits a certain kind of world and suggests certain ways of behaving in this world. Television wrestling exhibitions also reveal a good deal about the character of the people who watch it, even, as a matter of fact, of the people in certain regions or cities. For example, in America Mexican wrestlers in Los Angeles are villains but in San Francisco they are heroes. The same wrestler is "dirty" in Los Angeles and "clean" in San Francisco. Now I must confess that I have not watched a great deal of wrestling on television in England. The programs are presented with intimations of whimsy and the suggestion that one is to watch tomfoolery. This is not quite the case in America, or at least in the San Francisco-Oakland area of California. There the referee is introduced in a "solemn" manner, as having been "appointed" by some official body and being licensed by the state. The American wrestling matches have a great deal more to them. For example, wrestlers have to be "stick men;" they have to be good talkers (the stick being a microphone), and generally speaking there is a good deal of insulting and bad-mouthing in the between-match interviews. It isn't unusual for a good stick man to intimate he will kill his opponent, or leave him a bloody pulp - as well as to claim that he is clean and good and his opponent dirty and a "xxxx."

Frequently wrestlers give little orations in some "native" tongue to their admirers, so it is useful to know Spanish, German, Polish, Italian, Greek, Arabic, and a few other languages to properly appreciate a wrestling match. And American wrestling matches have flair. There are now (since Gorgeous George) an astonishing number of heroes and anti-heroes: American Indians (usually called Chief something or other), beautiful blonde supermen, nasty Germans and Russians, sly Indians with "cobra holds" as well as gigantic Negroes, fat hillbillies (Haystax Calhoun weighs 600 pounds) and innumerable other freaks, masters, strongmen, Golden Boys, and Adonis types.

There are also, of course, women, dwarf women, dwarf men, and sometimes there are team matches, with four or six wrestlers performing. Almost every wrestler in America has certain holds from which there is no escape; what are called "submission holds." The bad guys frequently rely on simplicities such as choking, eye gouging, strangling, rubbing one's opponents eyes along the ring ropes or breaking a chair over his back, hair pulling, judo cuts (which are always lethal against pushovers but don't seem to have any effect on heroes and winners) and various other punishments. The moral universe of wrestling is quite simplistic: usually there is a "good guy" and a "bad guy", and frequently it is the bad guy who wins, though not always. Certain good guys (Golden Boys) almost always win, after they lose their temper and become "dirty," giving the villain a bit of his own medicine, and frequently a bit more, just for good measure.

All of this is done with hoopla. Everyone in America knows it is "fake," that wrestling isn't a sport and that these wrestlers (most of whom are college boys from the mid-west) are really superb actors. Of course they do hurt one another from time to time, but since a top wrestler earns £40,000 a year, for wrestling three or four times a week, it is worth the risk.

Now what is remarkable about English wrestling is that it is so blunt and unimaginative. It lacks charismatic individuals, it lacks "flash," it lacks structure. It is terribly dull: it is like boiled meat--you get some nourishment, but it doesn't taste very good. When I watch wrestling and when deal with some people here I can hardly refrain from shouting "clods...get on with it for Christ's sake! " What I'm screaming for is a bit of color and style; I do not think you can expect it from the average Englishman. To see the difference between the way wrestling is presented in America and England examine the chart below:

BRITISH TV WRESTLING	AMERICAN TV WRESTLING
Small ring	Big ring
Little theatricality	Much theatricality
Referee's status is ambiguous	Referee represents state
Wrestlers dull generally	Charismatics, freaks
Mildly violent	Very violent
Crowd not important	Crowd very important
Rounds and falls	Falls

The very size of the ring inhibits the action. In the small British ring it is hard to create the drama you get in American rings, which are larger as a rule. And generally the audience is much closer, so that wrestlers can be thrown onto the people when tossed out of the ring. You also don't get as bloodthirsty an audience in British television broadcasts. In America it is frequent for little old grey-haired grand- motherly women to come rushing to the ring shouting "kill him, kill him"as they urge their heroes on.

The wrestlers here also haven't much of a sense of drama. In America the matches tend to have structure, building up to frenetic moments when bodies are flying all around the ring and there is great excitement. Most of the time in America you can sense when a match will be ending; after the good guy and bad guy have each got their licks in there comes the moment for resolution--probably agreed upon before-hand by both the participants. English matches seem to have no resolutions; someone gets a hold or pins his opponent and that is that.

In one match I saw in England, a "popular" Italian wrestler defeated an unpopular Englishman, who was some kind of a champion. No sooner had the Englishman been pinned, after a bit of dirty wrestling, than he left the ring and disappeared. In America there would have been protests, perhaps other things? You can never tell. Frequently a dirty wrestler, after he has left his opponent lying unconscious or unable to move, will go over and kick him a few times and "inflict" a bit more punishment on him, to irritate the audience.

Now it might be argued, "look how much more humane we are. Our wrestlers are moderately dirty, have a sense of civility," and all that. But my point is that wrestling here is not much of an entertainment, is bloodlessly (not bloody) boring compared with its American counterpart, and is probably a fairly accurate mirror of English culture or, at least, the culture of the man in the street here. Style, charisma, theatricality-- all of these things are reserved for a small elite of upper-middle class and upper class people, just like in the medieval days when there were churls and peasants (clods) and a small aristocracy ruling by "divine right." In England wrestling on the telly is but a pale simulacrum of America's simulated madness in the ring, but it is an accurate mirror of the character of its audience.

DRIVING IN ENGLAND

It is a grey, overcast day in London, the kind of day that I imagine is typical in the winter here. I find myself somewhat ambivalent about my stay. On the one hand London is an exciting and remarkable city, and we have lots of friends and acquaintances, and there is plenty to do. Yet, I find myself plagued with minor irritations all the time which tend to make me a bit despondent. It is quite irrational, I know, but that is beside the point.

It so happens that my mind works symbolically and I tend to read meaning into little, trivial, commonplace matters and things. This book may be thought of, in a sense, as a study in the significance and secret meaning of the insignificant and commonplace. I have a little drawing I frequently make of myself, as a secret agent, in search of the obvious.

This morning I was invited out for tea at a friend's house near Wembley. I had purchased the A to Z Map of London and the DeLuxe A to Z Atlas and Index of London. I had planned the trip as carefully as a general might plan a campaign, and yet I got lost both going and coming back. My wife was sitting beside me, scouting and helping with the directions, but it was hard to find my way because streets are inadequately marked in England. Somehow, it is "assumed" that you know where you are and where you are going--a carryover, perhaps, of the provincialism that characterizes this land.

The lights or direction signals are also inadequate. The British don't seem to have discovered the green arrow, so that when trying to get off the North Circular road I found it necessary to wait for various lights to change, and a break in traffic to occur, before I could swing off. I find that driving in London (and I avoid it as much as I can) leaves me in a state of nervous shock and near collapse.

I find it quite remarkable that Britain has poured millions of pounds into a supersonic jetliner, and leaves its road system in such a primitive level of development. I would estimate that except for a few super highways the British are about twenty years behind the times in terms of road-building technology and everything that goes with it. Many cars do not have seatbelts or headrests (which reduce whiplash). There seems to be little concern for such things for some reason. In America, all new cars have had to have both for some years now; new cars in Britain must have seatbelts now, which is a move in the right direction; To carry my peasant/prince thesis a bit further here, it seems to me that when the common people are involved, little attention is paid (by the powers that be) to their comfort and security. Peasants aren't worth bothering with in the princely mind. It is not that the British couldn't make more signs, insist upon safety features in cars, and modernize their road system; it is that all of this doesn't seem quite worth the bother. And so the peasants in their minis struggle onward against the lights, managing, somehow, to get where they want, with a considerable amount of discomfort and requiring a great deal of ingenuity and, at times, foolhardy courage.

SHOPPING CARTS, SUPERMARKETS, AND THE SUPERSTRUCTURE

I find that most of the English people have a very strong identification with England, its history and culture. They may be the moral equivalent (nowadays) of peasants, but seem to think they are blessed by England's glories, and that the existence of royalty and of princes is some kind of a benefit.

Of course I am speaking metaphorically here. W. H. Auden
has said "Each in the prison of himself is convinced of his own
freedom," and the same could apply to national fantasies. We
are. all, deep within us, convinced that our customs, our
beliefs, our lifestyles, and our ways. of doing things are best.

Thus when I mentioned, in a lecture on one occasion, that I
thought that one of the supreme symbols of life in England is
the little shopping cart that legions of women drag behind then
every day, and that the way people shop in England was
wasteful (of time) there was a great outcry in the audience.
"What's the hurry?" said one person. "What will you do with
the time saved?" "Who likes frozen meat?" asked another.
People started making impassioned speeches about the English
way of life and why refrigerators aren't necessary.

Comparisons are, of course, odious; there is always the
implication of judgment at the very least, and criticism is not
palatable to anyone. Yet I must say that I believe the British
(and European, for it is not restricted to Britain) way of
purchasing food to be quite irrational. Millions of women are
out to millions of stores wasting millions of hours every day.
Shopping is a way of life in England and though it has certain
values, in that it provides a means for socialization and enables
women to "get out of the house" for a while, it also means that
they are enslaved. Daily shopping is a necessity! You miss a
day (or forget about an early closing) and you starve!

England is a nation of shopkeepers, but the other side of that is that it is also a nation of shoppers. The multiplicity of shops is astonishing and in each shop are large numbers of clerks whose productivity, I would imagine, is relatively low. I must say I find it all rather quaint and in a sense "charming," but it is not very efficient.

The American institution which contrasts with the multiplicity of little shops in England is the supermarket, though there are now supermarkets here, and even, in fact, an American one-- Safeway. Powerful forces have led to the development of the supermarket in America. It is a supremely rationalized institution, it is relatively efficient, it provides numerous services for its customers, it brings together an astonishing assortment of goods under one roof and it is the modern equivalent of a street market except that it is located in one building. Supermarkets in America are getting larger and larger now. The typical American supermarket used to stock 4000 products; it now stocks 10,000 and its volume has grown greatly. The larger the supermarket the larger the volume (and the volume may increase almost geometrically) and the greater the profits.

The consumer in Britain is under the illusion that all these shops are a convenience for him. In reality he pays dearly for them, in time and money. The shops reflect a kind of anarchy that pervades: this country- There is no reason, no order, and no organization to speak of. Instead the streets are lined with little shops that replicate each other every five blocks, and, for the most part, are not particularly interesting.

Thus the woman out with her cart is a kind of beast of burden…a coolie, a carrier, who is tied to these shops by invisible threads that bind her as securely as if they were steel chains. "My grocer," they say, or "my greengrocer," but this "my" has a kind of reciprocal obligation to it. She "belongs" to them as much, really, as they "belong" to her.

I have a particular animus against these shopping carts because, as wielded by many women, they are often dangerous weapons. I happen to do most of the shopping in England at the local Waitrose (the significance of the name is apparent-- you wait and by the time you get to the cashier you find the price of everything rose) and have been wounded numerous times by these carts. For some reason people seem to bump into each other frequently here. I can't explain it. The supermarket has narrow aisles, for one thing, and people seem to rush about in it, for another. But even outside the market there seems to be little concern for other people's territory.

The shopping cart is a symbol which embraces what might be called the system of consumption and involves, ultimately, the economic system in Britain and the continent. Economics means, literally, the laws of the household and there is m direct connection between the shopping cart and the household appliances people own (no refrigerator or a miniscule one without a freezing suction of any significance means no frozen foods means there is a need each day for fresh food, and so on). In turn there is a connection between the wages people get, how much they can afford to spend at any one time , and how stores operate. All of this, in turn, relates to the proportion of people who have cars and whether or not supermarkets have parking lots and the way goods are packaged and the kinds of paper bags available.

It may be that the American supermarket represents, when pushed to its ultimate state, a kind of extreme, antiseptic, overwhelming, supremely rationalized, impersonal, institution, but I do not think this is an accurate picture at all. The gigantic supermarket currently popular in America represents consumption at the highest level of rationality and efficiency, and if it is an extreme, so might I add is the anarchistic continental system of consumption. The supermarket could not function the way it does without the American my of life, the American economy, American affluence, the American passion for efficiency and time-saving.

The supermarket is as generalist institution; the private shopping cart and all it involves is an artifact of a "specialized" mode of consumption. The shopping cart is for people with tunnel vision, immediate needs, present-mindedness. It is the legacy of the peasant, the little man who makes little purchases; In order to move, into the era of the supermarket and all it stands for there needs to be a wide-ranging revolution all up and down British society; you cannot impose super-marketing as a total system without restructuring the rest of society to go along with it.

THE UNDERGROUND DIAGRAM 0F LONDON:
IS KNOWLEDGE POWER?

There is probably no work of art that strangers in London spend more time looking at than the map of the London Underground, designed by one Paul E. Garbutt. Native Londoners or people who have lived there at long time and who travel on the underground have memorized or internalized large sections of it, and don't have to bother with it; but for others, it is a diagram of compelling interest.

I really don't know what to call it. Actually, it isn't a map, since it was consciously designed and is diagrammatic rather than representational. It is formal and abstract, perhaps both a piece of hard-edge realism (out of the Mondrian school) and a functional tool. There is no concern with streets or with scale, and yet the diagram is terrifically powerful. This may be because it is total. It "comprehends" so to speak the entire system, which is enormous.

The London Transport calls it a "Diagram of Lines" (which sounds plebeian yet which has an art nouveau ring about it) but it is quite obviously much more than that. The roundel, the circle with a line through it, is a potent symbol, a kind of variation on the Chinese Yin and Yang symbol, and the diagram itself, covering about 250 miles of track, is a model, of economy and functionality. The roundel is a symbol of "undergroundness" in general and the diagram is a symbol, at a lower level of abstraction, of the underground as an entity or as a system with its eight different lines, interchanges, etc. The diagram is both a symbol and a guide and provides what might be called representational mastery. I have mentioned that the underground contains approximately 250 miles of track. To understand the scope of this system, you might compare it with the Bay Ares Regional Transport (BART) in the San Francisco-Oakland area, which will have 75 miles of track and which hopes to function (if they can ever get it finished and working properly) as a regional transportation system. The statistics provided by the London Transport are impressive:

mileage in tunnel 99 miles
longest continuous tunnel 17 miles
longest journey without change 34.1 miles
number of stations 279
speed 20.3 miles per hour

The figure for speed is not impressive; however, when contrasted with the average speed of buses in London (11.3 miles per hour) it doesn't seem too bad.

Now what is remarkable is that all of the above is "comprehended" in innumerable printed diagrams of every size and coloration, provided by London transport, tourist guides, etc. The diagram gives mastery and power; it is functional and provides one with the illusion of control, somehow, of this vast entity. Of course this sense of power is contingent; you can only go where the transport goes, and in frequent cases (especially for the north of London) it is hard to get from one place to another.

For example, if you wish to go from Hampstead, on the Northern line, to Wembley Park, on the Bakerloo line, you must go nine stops south on the Northern line to pick up a train and go twelve stops north on the Waterloo line. Yet Hampstead and Wembley Park are quite near one another. (You could save a couple of stops by changing cars twice and maneuvering about, but I don't imagine it is worth the effort.)

The key to the underground is the interchange system. Since the underground was. not built as one system, but represents a merger of a number of formerly separate ones, it contains numerous redundancies. It is held together by the interchanges which connect one, two or three of the eight different lines. In a sense the underground is really a regional system, since its focus is in bringing people into the center of London, and getting them about in the downtown area; of the city and not facilitating their getting about in the extremities. There are something like forty interchanges, and most of them are located in or near the central loop 'formed by the Circle line (and at times the District and Metropolitan lines).

Had the underground been planned and the same. amount of track utilized without the wasted repetitions, a much better coverage of the outer regions, perhaps by some kind of a northern and southern ring, might have been effected. Nevertheless, despite the redundancies and certain inconveniences, the underground is an effective system. It serves as a reference point for people; you tell people where you live by citing the nearest underground station, and this station becomes part of a person's identity, actually. A person who lives near the Hampstead tube is perceived as (if not really) different from a. person who lives near Elephant and Castle.

The tube stop becomes a central point in knowing the location of restaurants, cinema, theatres and museums. In part this is because it is hard to drive in London and find places to park, but also because of the power of the Underground Diagram to place things in people's minds.

Think of it. The greater London area has a population that is probably in excess of 10 million people and yet the locations of most places in this city are presented in a highly abstract and formalized diagram that often is no larger than four by six inches. A vast and complicated system serving ten million people presented in a simple little diagram which enables anyone to understand it in moments. Though it takes hardly any time to master the diagram, it often takes a good deal of time to get from one place to another, which demonstrates that the Underground Diagram confers the illusion, but not the reality, of power. Because we understand the system we think we control it. Knowledge may be power, but not in the case of the London Underground.

MAD ENGLISHMEN

This afternoon we had lunch at our next door neighbor's, the H's, and a very fine and fancy lunch it was. We had a joint of lamb, roast potatoes, cabbage, a superb apple pie and excellent coffee. It took three hours altogether, and we had a fascinating conversation. On the basis of this conversation I have definitely concluded that some eight out of every ten

Englishmen and Englishwomen are slightly mad.

The word mad is not used here, of course. People are described as peculiar, odd, strange, funny, bizarre, and eccentric. But there is always something peculiar, odd, etc. about everyone. One neighbor is an orthodox Jew, and asked Mrs. H. to wind her alarm clock one Friday evening. When she didn't arrive when they expected, the woman's husband knocked on the wall (he couldn't use the bell, for that would be "work" and against the Torah, presumably) and barged in, yelling "the clock, the clock." Mr. H., who knew nothing of the agreement, was astounded; his wife had told him nothing about the arrangement, and there was considerable chaos and confusion all around, until she arrived in the middle, to straighten things out.

Almost everyone I've met in England seems to think that almost everyone else is slightly "daft," to use a common tern. It is simply remarkable how free people are with their negative assessments of other people. What is amusing about this is that everyone becomes caught in the web that they each spin. You can be invited to someone's home for tea and each member of the family will, in privacy, tell you all kinds of terrible things about each other member of the family. This one's "repressed," that one's a miser, another one "never had a woman in his life," and a fourth is simply "deranged."

In America we have a notion that eccentricity flowers in England, because English eccentrics are good "human interest" and because we have rather mad. notions about the English. After all, it was an Englishman, Noel Coward, who taught us that "mad dogs and Englishmen go out in the midday sun". It probably is true that the ambiance in England is, in a certain sense, so permissive, that people can pursue their passions into eccentricity without being hampered too much.

This is because England is an elitist society and in elite societies privileged members are allowed to pursue their whims without being subjected to the crushing force of conformity, which is so strong in egalitarian countries such as America. In America there is great pressure placed upon people; to be different is to imply one is better, and that will not do. There is, of course, an anti-establishment subculture in America which pursues its individuality to such lengths that it becomes mannered and precious. Different forms of revolt are also captured by the media and commercialized for fun and profit on all sides.

All of this badmouthing which one finds in England is really a form of aggression. Because the culture here does not sanction physical violence (except for certain cases, such as that perpetrated by schoolmasters on children) the English assuage their need for release by being gossips and scandalmongers and saying nasty things about one another. Americans may think terrible things about one another but they do not seem to say terrible things about each other to the extent that the English do. This may explain why the English have developed such remarkable verbal facility amongst the educated and literate elements of society. The masses have few and rather limited things to say about one another, but the classes exploit the vocabulary of psychoanalysis, husbandry and any number of fields, all with an aura of factuality and objectivity that helps them mask their evil intents even from themselves.

A YEAR AMONGST THE UK:
AN ANTHROPOLOGICAL EXTRAVAGANZA

I don't know how it was that I ended up amongst the UK, but circumstances led me to live with them and observe their various and sundry rituals (as Malinowski said, "ritual is always rite") to study their dominant myths, to chart their everyday activities--in short to do what any fieldworker does when living amongst strange peoples. The UK, once a savage and bloodthirsty people, are now relatively civilized. They are found on two rain-soaked islands, near the continent of Eur, and are much ridiculed by the people in Eur for their habit of boiling meat and serving beer warm.

The UK are a confederation comprising four tribes: the Eng (known for their strange little black derbies which they call bowlers), the Sco (famous because the men wear skirts), the Wa and the Nirl. Although these four tribes speak the same language, *Englingua,* because of the incredible variations in the way they speak it many of them cannot understand one another. Still, there are certain phrases that are universally used, such as "Gaw Blimey" and "Wot?" and "here, here," sometimes pronounced "ere, ere."

One of the favorite pastimes of the UK is in telling myths and legends about their kings and queens. One king is said to have had eight wives; when one displeased him he had her head out off. ("Off with your maidenhead," he said. Then "Off with your head, maiden"). A war was supposedly fought over which end of the egg--the big end or the little end--one opens when eating a soft boiled egg. The UK like nothing better than going to plays about their kings and seeing them cut their wives' heads off and throw one another into dungeons.

The islands on which the UK live are full of old castles and fortresses and people visit them to see the dungeons where various kings, queens, princes and bishops were imprisoned and killed. That was the national sport before the development of roc and soc, their two preoccupations now. The UK still have a king and queen, mostly to dedicate underground stations and endorse brands of marmalade and tinned peas. All kings and queens have to love horses or else they are thrown into a dungeon.

In the old days the kings and their friends, the royalty, used to ride around covered in tin cans and have tournaments, in which they would poke at each other with big sticks or try to hack one another to bits with long metal things which were primitive forms of can openers. One king who liked round tables. is especially famous for having killed numerous dragons and monsters that used to inhabit the land. (He was so successful that none are to be seen at this time.)

The sport which the UK follow most passionately, soc, is not unique to them, though they presume themselves to be the best soc players in the world. Soc is a sport in which people kick a round ball all about a big field and chase it about, and hit it a great deal with their heads. It is here that the thick heads of the UK are a great advantage. Old soc players are generally thrown in dungeons and beheaded, so many resign when young and become milkmen, butchers and, if lucky, plumbers. When the UK lost a big soc match to a rival tribe, the Pol, one of their papers had for a headline, "The End of the World!"

The UK worship a god who is, they imagine, very much like themselves, in that he speaks *Englingua* and takes boiled water and leaves (tea) at ten in the morning and four in the afternoon. They worship this god in big buildings which they erected many years ago, and which hardly anybody visits now except tourists (who want to see where certain kings were killed) and lonely old ladies. These halls are convenient places to purchase postcards and catch cold.

VATICAN

Now the UK no longer build big buildings for their gods, but build big stadiums and airports. This is so people who wish to fly to visit the UK and see where UK kings were killed can do so easily. (The most famous place to see dungeons and where more kings, queens, ladies and little boys were killed is called the Tower, and many people visit it each year.) In the soc stadiums the best soc players in UK run around for endlessly long periods of time and manage to score one or two goals, sometimes three, during a game. The soc stadiums are also used for roc concerts in which bands of school leavers and functional illiterates play electric guitars and entertain young girls, known as teenyboppers and teenyweenyboppers, and young men known as mods, rockers and skinheads.

The UK are notorious for having sour dispositions, which accounts or their loving candy, or as they call them, "sweets." Also, the UK are terrible gossips and say the most horrible things about one another at their morning and afternoon teas. They also believe in beating children in schools with canes and birch branches. At the age of eleven, all children are given futures by their teachers. Some are sent off to Oxbridge, a famous university where they are required to punt, play a game called rugger, and write books of philosophy. Others are sent off to be milkmen, dustmen and bobbies. When not delivering milk or picking up dust, these types, in the working classes, as they call themselves, play soc or indulge in their favorite pastime "go wn' out". They assemble in huge mobs, carry signs and make speeches. Since the working classes and the Oxbridgeans who run the country speak different *Englingua,* they have to spend a good deal of time talking to one another before they understand each other. While all this is going on, the Primi and the MOP's who operate the government while the king and queen are opening subways and eating marmalade, make speeches and have meetings and drive around in big black limousines, called Minis.

UK women are notoriously ugly. Some have long thin noses that wiggle while they speak; others have snub noses and mousey features. (They all manage to get married, however, because they can boil meat.) They consider it fashionable to wear rags and old garments which they get from dustmen. A few wear skirts called micro-minis, which are, in reality, skirts they used to wear in the third form. The only good looking women in UK are the au pair girls, imported from all over the world to look after UK children while their mothers are out washing their horses' behinds, attending charity teas or selling fish.

Some of the UK, whose great grandparents were usually crooks and swindlers, and who are rich, love to chase foxes. The UK do not believe it is fair to have one UK chase one fox, since foxes are notoriously clever. Therefore usually fifty UK mounted on horseback and a hundred hounds, chase a fox to equalize the odds. The hunt ends when the dogs tear the fox to pieces, after which the UKs on the hunt have tea. and cucumber sandwiches, discuss the UK's glorious heritage and various interesting problems of moral philosophy and complain about the cost of servants.

It is best to have gone to Oxbridge and studied linguistic philosophy if you wish to chase foxes, though the very best preparation to join the Queen's Guard after Oxbridge and march around in little soldier suits and learn how to be wooden soldiers. The Queen's Guard protect her while she is in the kitchen eating bread and honey and on her way to underground stations. After the Queen's Guard, Oxbridgers marry girls who have studied poetry and ballet in fancy private academies called Comprehensive Schools and go into business to make a fortune, so they can wear top hats when they chase foxes.

All in all I would have to say the UK are amongst the most crazy people on the face of the earth, and certainly the most pernicious, at least as far as foxes are concerned.

THE QUEEN'S TOY SOLDIERS: ARE THEY LUCKY STIFFS?

During the first part of my stay in England I took my family to see the Changing of the Guard. It was mobbed with tourists from all over the world, who were packed solid around the gates and across the street on various statues and the steps leading to the Mall. Platoons of camera-laden Japanese flowed about, and you could hear German, Spanish and any number of languages being spoken.

Why all these people were there is a question that interests me. Everyone knows, of course, that "the British know how to put on a good show," and the Changing of the Guard has a hint of splendor and grandeur about it, but I find it a very thin event and not worth the effort it took to get to Buckingham palace. It is free and that may account for its wide popularity.

There was one thing that struck me, however, and that was a guard inside the palace grounds who stood at attention without moving (so it seemed) as much as an eyelid. He seemed to be frozen into his stance and might just as well have been a wooden soldier carved by some master craftsman. Many of the tourists standing around me, outside the gate, marveled at him. "How does he do it?" they asked. A better question might be-- what does it mean to have a man turn into a toy soldier? To me he symbolized the oppressive weight of tradition and formalism that I sense in England, and a kind of self-control that verges on the pathological. I assume that the men who serve as guards engage in a kind of self-hypnosis that allows them to maintain their rigid position the way they do. But the adjectives one might use to describe these guards are all, ultimately, quite negative: frozen, rigid, like a statue, motionless, etc. There is a ring of morbidity to it all--a kind of rigor mortis, but for the living and not the dead.

Why should guards be rigid and seemingly lifeless? Why should they approximate toy soldiers? Is there any value in having a guard motionless and stiff, like a board? These guards symbolize and concretize (a good word since they seem to be made of concrete, seem almost to be cast rather than being made of flesh and blood) the most negative aspects of English. They symbolize the suppression of instinct, of warmth, of humanity.

They are like marionettes which have been tossed, by chance, into a certain position, and which remain there until someone pulls a string or two. Self-control is an admirable feature, but carried to such lengths as one finds in the guards, it is monstrous and brutalizing. If, as I have been told, it is considered a great honor to serve in the guard, and an honor more or less reserved for people with "good blood" and Oxbridge educations, then all the worse I say.

Of course I come from a. culture which does not have such traditions, which stresses being "down to earth", informal, ordinary and flexible. In America we believe, as the song goes, in "different strokes for different folks." We don't put on good parades the way the English do, because we know that we have the power, and don't need the pomp. But what I am concerned with is not the power of the guard (except as a symbol) but the power of a culture and tradition that leads people to want to become guards, and that makes approximating a toy soldier an honor. I will, no doubt, be accused of reductionism, of not being aware of the traditions behind the guards, of what their stance signifies, and that sort of thing. One can always make such arguments, but I don't accept the logic. If you have to be a "true believer" to properly understand anything, then nothing will be criticized since "true believers" are not critical. These guards, most certainly, are true believers with as much faith (is that the word?) as any Hindu fakir who puts himself into a trance. England, I would suggest, needs people who have a sense of the way things are moving and who can help shape that movement; what they get is a genius for standing still becoming one of the highest attributes in their "best" young men.

McDONALD'S AND WIMPY'S:
A TALE OF TWO HAMBURGERS
(Published in *New.Society*, Jan. 10, 1974)

Ten years ago, when I had my first McDonald's hamburger, I sensed that somehow I was in the presence of an enormous force, an institution of awesome energy. McDonald's hamburger is, it turns out, an evangelical hamburger, a hamburger with grandiose territorial ambitions as well as divine zeal. In the course of the last decade it has become the dominant" fast-food" franchise in America and it is now spreading abroad, carrying its gospel of machine technology wedded to cheap hamburgers wherever it can find a mouth-hold, and converting whomever it can to the glories of junk food, American style.

The genius of the McDonald's hamburger is organization, rationalization, and specialization, all carried to the point of perfection, so that the consumer can have his hamburger with the minimum delay and at the cheapest price possible. There is now even a McDonald's "University" where McDonald owners are taught how to operate their restaurants super-efficiently. These franchises, which offer a very restricted menu, work on a continuous-flow format, something like an automobile assembly-line, with hamburgers being cooked continually, and everything else being at the ready, so that orders are filled almost. instantaneously. The secret is being able to estimate demand, so that no hamburgers, are wasted; this is possible because the operation is supremely rational and efficient, and because human beings are, in the mass, predictable within certain limits.

Below the individual mouth lurks the mass stomach, and McDonald's understands this stomach as does nobody else in America--and perhaps the world. McDonald's offers a machine-tooled hamburger, a hamburger that is in truth more of an abstraction than a reality, one that is all essence and without corporeality. What do you expect for 20 cents (8p)--meat? You do not eat a McDonald's hamburger because you are hungry, though four or five of their cheapies and some chips might fill you up. You eat them because McDonald's offers immediate "gratification" and also assuages your command imperatives. When you eat a McDonald's hamburger you feel that you are part of America and in communion with all the vitality as well as diabolical forces at work there.

You do not get this feeling when you eat a Wimpy burger. Wimpy provides an undistinguished, even regrettable hamburger. Mine was a thin wafer, pale grey, verging on brown, that lay uncomfortably upon a few soggy fried onions. The roll it came in had the faintest hint of a crust and was Just slightly more substantial than the McDonald's roll, which is like cotton fluff. But we must remember that the Wimpy burger at eleven pence for a take-away hamburger, costs twice as much as an American over-the-counter one. My particular hamburger had a coarse grain and two extras: it had a sizeable piece of gristle in it, as well as (somehow) a piece of thread about two inches long. I had ordered one take-out Wimpy burger, and as the cook passed it to me, in a small bag, I had none of the feeling you get at a McDonald's. Wimpy is not really a fast-food house; it is a restaurant that happens to sell lousy hamburgers. (I don't know what the other food at Wimpy's is like, but I am not tempted to try my luck a second time.) So, in a sense, it is unfair to compare Wimpy and McDonald's.

Wimpy is named after a gluttonous character in the old American comic strip Popeye, and that's about as far as the Wimpy bar goes in resembling anything "American." In America the fast-food joints are plastic, all right, but they are authentically and outrageously plastic; they take delight in their vulgarity and push it at times to the point of being art. Wimpy, on the other hand, and its competitors (pancake houses, egg houses, etc.) have a diluted garishness that is not, in any way, exciting. So Wimpy doesn't have the symbolic richness that McDonald's does; it does not carry its psychological baggage and does not confer any kind of psychic reinforcement upon its customers.

And, relatively speaking, the essential Wimpy burger is frightfully expensive. For sixteen pence you don't get much value for money. There are, of course, all kinds of hamburgers, depending upon what you want to pay for them. In London now there are many "American" hamburger joints which offer thick, charcoal-broiled hamburgers, but they are for aristocratic types with bulging wallets. They taste much better than Wimpy's and McDonald's products and in some cases oven work out to be, relatively speaking, less expensive. Wimpy and McDonald's produce hamburgers for the mass man, for the person in a hurry or the insolvent student, for the man without qualities who wants a hamburger without qualities. Wimpy offers a bare hamburger devoid of condiments, except for fried onions; McDonald's, on the other hand, insists-,you take your hamburger with some kind of a mixture of mustard and relish and tomato catsup, though f you protest I have heard you can get a hamburger without "the works."

But Wimpy and McDonald's, and all their imitators and competitors, have a grander significance that must be explained. I am referring to the *hamburgeoisement* of the masses, which is especially evident in McDonald's. The automated hamburger is marching, ineluctably, into the cuisine of the western world, and as it does, it usurps the place held by traditional foods in various countries. It is changing people's eating habits and with this, the whole social fabric which has been built around those eating patterns. The basic function of the automated hamburger is mystification--fooling people into believing that they have eaten meat and making them think they are postmodern.

In America people eat more meat than ever before, but statistics show that since the second world war they are eating much less steak and other prime cuts and much more hamburger, so in truth their standard of living has gone down. Curiously enough, the fast food franchise (owner-operated hamburger stand) is the last hope of the so-called "little American" to rise in the world. The service industries is where most of the growth is in the American economy now, but there is now so much competition between hamburger joints or hamburger mansions (some are quite fancy now) that the hamburger no longer guarantees wealth and success. All too often, on both the individual and on the national level, it only leads to indigestion and heartburn as well as heartache.

What I have been trying to suggest is that the McDonald's and Wimpy hamburgers must be seen as more than mere hamburgers. They are potent symbols which comprehend within them, whole societies, economic systems, and a host of other things. The digestive system and the socio-economic system meet at the hamburger system. Remarkable, isn't it, what you find in chopped meat sometimes?

WHAT MAKES PEOPLE LAUGH?
A VISIT WITH BARRY TOOK

Early in my stay - it may have been September or October -
there a program on the BBC dealing with humor. The purpose
of the program was to explain why we laugh, a subject I find
most compelling. I watched it—it was written and given by
someone named Barry Took, but found it quite disappointing.
This was because the program lacked structure and because
Took didn't take his analysis far enough. Being in a
flamboyant mood I decided to write to him and propose that I
help him do a program which would carry on where he left the
ball, and give a better analysis of the nature of humor. I had
my catalogue of the basic techniques of humor which we
could use as the basis of a program. Actually, I didn't have a.
program in mind ... that is, I had no conception of doing a
program. What I thought was that I might be able to help him
do a. better one himself.

I wrote him a brief note explaining something about my work
on humor and asking whether we might meet, to talk about our
mutual interest. Nothing happened for a couple of weeks and I
forgot all about the matter, but at the end of November I got a;
call from him and we got together at the BBC on the 26th. It's
hard to say how old Took is…in his late forties or early fifties,
perhaps. He has grey hair and thick dark glasses. He met me in
the lobby of the BBC tower and led me up to his office, a

sparsely furnished room with a couple of wooden desks, chairs, and a bookcase with some material filed haphazardly in it.

We talked for more than three hours and managed, I think, to get to know each other tolerably well. We started by talking about humor. I showed him my glossary of the techniques of humor and explained how my work differed from the work of most of the people who wrote on humor, in that I wasn't interested in why people laugh. Rather I was concerned with what makes them laugh, and accordingly had made a content analysis, of sorts, of humor and classified the techniques that various humorists used, so that people could understand how humor works, so to speak.

1. Absurdity	16. Embarrassment	31. Parody
2. Accident	17. Exaggeration	32. Puns
3. Allusion	18. Exposure	33. Repartee
4. Analogy	19. Facetiousness	34. Repetition
5. Before and After	20. Grotesque	35. Reversal
6. Bombast	21. Ignorance	36. Ridicule
7. Burlesque	22. Imitation	37. Rigidity
8. Caricature	23. Impersonation	38. Sarcasm
9. Catalogue	24. Infantilism	39. Satire
10. Chase Scene	25. Insults	40. Scale, Size
11. Coincidence	26. Irony	41. Slapstick
12. Comparison	27. Literalness	42. Speed
13. Definition	28. Mimicry	43. Stereotypes
14. Disappointment	29. Mistakes	44.Theme/Var.
15. Eccentricity	30. Misunderstanding	45. Unmasking

Techniques of Humor in Alphabetical Order

He seemed to be quite interested in this. He had, as all humorists and gag writers have done, intuitively arrived at many of the techniques I listed and explained in my glossary, but being a "natural" and not having elaborated his ideas to any extent (and he didn't articulate others) he couldn't push his analysis far enough so his program had failed. It had a disastrous format: he talked in a studio and showed examples of things, like a professor giving a lecture. Programs about humor almost always fail, as a matter of fact.

This did not particularly bother him, for one of the things he kept repeating was that he had "room to fail" and that he felt it was better to take chances, sometime, and fail, than put on a program which would have a guaranteed level of adequacy, but which was nothing exceptional. "I can always put on something safe that will work," he said, "but I'm free to fail. I can take risks from time to time." He said this was. because he was an unknown quantity at the BBC. At times he bad. put on shows that had received great acclaim and acceptance, and at other times he "bombed."

This matter of being "free to fail" is an important one. He didn't think television producers in America had that freedom since there was too much money riding on every program, and the commercialism in the American television industry tended to inhibit experimentation and novelty. I'm not so sure this is the case, but the fact that he had lots of room to play around in, in a mass medium, suggests» (to me, at least) that many of the axioms we learn about mass culture are not valid.

Everything need not appeal to the mythical "lowest common denominator." Our discussion turned to English society, a. subject dear to my heart, since I'm living in England and trying to decipher English society. He, in turn, had spent three months in Les Angeles, as a gag writer for Rowan and Martin's "Laugh In," so we had a little session on comparative culture analysis. I described some of my "ordeals" in England and he said, "Yes, there is a lot of slack here," a word which I think is quite proper, and he described some of his ordeals with the BBC bureaucracy, which seems as inefficient as most bureaucracies.

I left him my glossary, by books *Pop Culture* and *The Comic-Stripped American*, and he said something about there being a chance that I might be, given some late-evening time on the BBC to put on a program.

"I'll speak with some of my friends here, who might help you with technical matters, and if they are interested you might get some time some evening. You won't make much, but it might be interesting."

"The money doesn't interest me," I replied. "I have never done things because they would make money; in fact, most of the work I've done has been considered as eccentric, trivial or cranky," I added. And with that he kicked no out of his office, because he had another appointment, and I wandered back to Golders Green.

I could not help but wonder about the place of chance and coincidence in life. If I had not seen his program (someone called my attention to it, as a matter of fact) and had not written to him, and if he had not answered, we might never have got together. When we did, we found that we had many interests. and ideas in common. This might be expected, since we are both involved, one way or another, with humor. I study it, analyze it, and at times use it; he makes it, or does the best he can in that regard. The BBC TV center, in the western part of London, is an ugly piece of British-modern architecture. A big round building that rises up, but which does not have particularly interesting shape to it. The blocking is all wrong. In that building sit writers grinding out teleplays, one after the other; journalists and documentary makers, producing public-affairs programs (acme of exceptional quality) and in one office sits Barry Took, trying to figure out how to make people laugh.

THE DAILY CALENDAR:
THE FULLY BOOKED LIVES OF THE MIDDLE CLASSES

Recently I attended a meeting of a social committee of an organization which will remain anonymous-- a meeting which I found most instructive. There were about a dozen people at the meeting, mostly couples, except for myself. Before I attended the meeting I received an agenda in the mail, and on the. evening of the meeting I received a phone call to make sure I would be there. Lots of energy at work.

Their first order of business (the reading of the minutes was omitted because the secretary was ill) was a discussion of a questionnaire the committee was sending out, in an effort to find out what social activities members of the organization would be interested in. The matter was complicated, because there was a covering letter starting out "Dear Member" and ending "Yours truly." "Don't you think Yours Sincerely would be better?" asked one of the committee members. "No," answered the chairman. "A letter starting out with Dear Member is too impersonal, and I can't sign it sincerely."

Also, the mailing of 1300 letters and questionnaires takes a bit of doing and they had to decide how to manage it all. Someone even suggested the whole idea was a bad one. The head of the organization had not co-operated with the venture, it seems. He believed that questionnaires like that were quite useless, a waste of time and money and an invasion of people's privacy. But the chairman of the committee, a forceful and exuberant individual, was resolved to push on with the project. Once this matter was out of the way, the committee addressed itself to planning the social calendar for the rest of the year, up to the summer.

The committee was not quite certain of its mission - raising money or helping people to get to know one another better or both. It was decided to have a variety of events, at a number of different price ranges. There was to be a "Brain" game, in which people could answer questions at different tables, on various subjects. There was a lot of talk about how much this should cost.

Originally it was decided upon that it should cost one pound per person. However, the chairman mentioned that people had complained about the cost of events put on by "The Social and Functions Committee," so after a bit of discussion it was decided to lower the price to 50p per person. I can't recall whether they decided to make another appeal for certain charitable entity. One member objected to the practice of always making appeals. She thought it would be nice to have something in which people weren't pressured. Someone else, however, argued that the need was desperate, and people could well afford more money.

In addition to the "Brain" evening, the committee decided to have a bridge evening, and a party of some kind. Someone suggested they sponsor a night at the movies, and this was debated at length. Some thought that if an evening of film was held, it should be at the headquarters of the organization. Others felt there shouldn't be an evening of film, because it wasn't a socializing experience, and people didn't really mix at such evenings;" they merely were together, but no relationships ensued.

The biggest, problem of the meeting involved a "culinary experience" that the vice-chairman thought might be a good idea.

> "What do you mean by a culinary experience", one member asked.
>
> "A good feed, in essence," was the reply.
>
> "Can we get really good cooking for a lot of people ? I mean, can you have a really good meal that way'?" someone asked.
>
> "That's not necessary", answered another person. "He knows a cook who caters meals from time to time she's even cooked for Princess Margaret."
>
> "How much would this cost?"
>
> "Shall we say three pounds per person? That's not too much for a good feed," volunteered the man who had suggested the culinary experience.

The couple who knew the cook suggested they all go to her little restaurant in Hemel Hempstead, but the gas shortage put the damper on that idea. This couple also suggested that going to her restaurant wouldn't give a good idea of her capabilities, because she catered to the relatively unsophisticated tastes of her clientele.

Finally the committee decided to engage her to cater a private dinner party for themselves, so they could see how good she was. People thought that three pounds per person was reasonable, and someone volunteered to host it.

"When shall we have it?" someone asked. At that many of the committee members whipped out daily calendars to see when they would be free. It could not be this day because someone had to fly to Bucharest. It could not be another day because a couple were going to Denmark. After a number of stabs at a reasonable date everyone agreed that they had a free Sunday a month off and plans were made to see what could be done about getting the woman.

The time for the tea break arrived, and several men went down to fetch tea. During this time a number of Irish jokes were told, all based upon the "stupidity" of the Irishman. I gather that the Irishman occupies the same status in the English joke world as the Pole does in the American joke world. The jokes were expertly told and actually quite funny, being absurd and fantastic. Some of them were similar to American moron jokes, also. After tea time the committee wrapped things up, set a time for the next meeting and adjourned.

"Will you be coming?" asked the wife of the chairman. "Yes," I said. In its odd way the evening had. been quite fascinating and I wanted to see how things were resolved. One of the committee members asked me if I needed a lift home, and everyone said good evening to me as I left. I really don't know why I was asked to attend these meetings, except that I got cornered one evening at one of their events and I suppose it was actually a gesture meant to expand my social horizons, so to speak. Originally the meeting was to be held in a private home and arrangements had been made for me to be picked up and returned.

What impressed me most about the meeting is that it revealed certain aspects of middle-class life that both attract and repel me. The people in the committee were dedicated to providing something constructive for their organization, and worked quite hard at their task. They were also all extremely intelligent and many of them were quite witty. The meeting itself was a rather comedic one--lots of gags, comic performances, and joking about, in addition to the Irish jokes, that is.

But the thing that fascinated me most about it was the way so many of the people used their Daily Calendars. The woman sitting beside me had one, and I glanced at it ... full of things jotted down for each day.

The good life is the busy life, and a marked up, scribbled over Daily Calendar is the sign of a good life. This participation hunger is a kind of aggression, and reflects a hunger for activity that has several motivations.

(On one hand it is a kind of assertiveness, a passionate desire to suck the marrow of life as completely as possible. It is a form of greed that manifests itself in frenzied effort to fully book oneself "into life," in a manner of speaking.)

I can't help but think that such people are really very lonely and have inadequately developed inner resources. It may be that people who need to be with others all the time can't stand themselves? It may reflect an evasion of the self that we all manage to achieve, one way or the other.

The round of daily activities allows us (and perhaps even forces us) to focus our energy and attention on the outside world and prevents us from thinking very much about ourselves. The working classes and the upper classes also practice such evasions; there are many methods...drink, sports, the telly, the cinema, etc. etc. But the important thing is to avoid focusing attention upon the self, upon the self that is lingering there within us, kept down and rendered inaccessible.

We have sill heard that inside every fat man there is a thin nan, longing to get out. The same thing applies to all of us, though not in terms of being fat but in terms of a submerged self that we occasionally take notice of, but generally keep hidden-- from others as well as ourselves.

This submerged self asks philosophical questions about the meaning of our lives, the morality of our activities. We avoid this submerged self. Instead of writing books of philosophy we write up appointments in our Daily Calendars, and add up our activities in a calculus of hedonism and self-evasion.

Thus there are several histories of Britain being written at this moment (and histories of every country). There is the official history, of the doings of kings and prime ministers and great artists and military commanders. But there is also the anonymous, petty-bourgeois history being written in all the Daily Calendars printed up by Collins and W. H. Smith, the history of the middle classes. There may also be a history of the working class, and this history may shape the future (if the Marxists are right). But it may also be that the working classes have no history, that they merely are hidden away in the shadows, keeping . things going, so the middle classes and the ruling classes can have their social committees and Parliaments .

WHAT MAKES THE ENGLISH LAUGH:
TILL DEATH US DO PART

Till Death Us Do Part has been one of the most popular television comedies of the past few years — and certainly one of the most popular television programs of this period. It is now in its fourth series and still going strong, though some of the critics have suggested that it may have outlived its usefulness and no longer is as funny or remarkable as it once was. I can't judge the merits of these criticisms because I have not seen the other three series, but even my limited viewing of the most recent episodes is enough for me to grasp that it is a remarkable program.

It has, in fact, spawned an American "imitation" called *All in The Family* which was, in turn, the most popular American comedy of the past couple of years - and it is also being imitated elsewhere now.

The basic theme of the program involves the de-romanticizing and demythologizing of the poor. What we find is not some kind of noble savage or one of (as we say in America) "nature's noblemen," an unlearned but somehow wise and virtuous soul with an intuitive grasp of the meaning of life; a generous soul, a good democrat. What we find is a genuine grotesque, Alf Garnett, who is locked into mortal combat with his wife, another grotesque (but a much more humanized one than Alf) and his daughter and son-in-law, who are quite normal and who are diametrically opposed to everything Alf stands for.

The title of the show is most ambivalent. It has something to do with the marriage contract and with marriage conflict. There is a little world of people who share a small, run-down apartment and who fight, like children, about everything. It is a kind of fight to the death, a blood feud between members of the same family who enjoy it all, who can't avoid the cutting remark or the practical joke, who love and hate each other a great deal.

Alf Garnett is what is called, by the sociologists, "a working class authoritarian." He is a bigot, a racist who has contempt for Jews, Negroes, people of all color, members of the Labour party, and what he calls "bloody Wogs." He, himself, is a study in contradiction--a working class Tory, who can't understand what the members of the Conservative Party are talking about, but whose habits of deference carry him on. He digs the fancy types who would find him absolutely loathsome, and he wears a homburg to complement his cheap National Health Service glasses.

He is a grotesque, whose grotesquery mirrors the distortions in the society in which he finds himself. He fascinates, perhaps because he forces us, in some strange way, to see ourselves. Monsters like Alf, full of rage and fury, reflect all of us. How we would like to be able to insult people, to "vent our spleen" at people we don't like, to be irrational and luxuriate in malicious and absurd hatred. Alf is pure feeling in a country full of uptight people with monstrous super-egos, who cannot let themselves go and express their feelings, whether generous or not. There is a great deal of tension in the air in England over the matter of aggression (which explains why darts are so popular and the hunt) and in this carefully preserved sea of nervous tranquility old Alf Garnett is thrashing about, screaming bloody murder, a brilliant anti-hero who has the luxury of being able to hate, and, as a corollary, being able to feel. In a country full of repressed hysterics Alf Garnett is the ego ideal of millions. They don't know this, of course. And he pays a price: he is a fool, nobody takes him seriously, people laugh at him. Actually he provides a number of gratifications for his followers. As I suggested above, he speaks for their "secret souls" which would like to be free to admit their hatred (at times, at least) of people. But we get a double payoff from him, for in addition to getting the forbidden pleasure of aggression against ethnic groups and political parties we don't like (vicariously) through Alf, we then get the added pleasure of feeling legitimate aggression against Alf, the aggressor. He gives us good "value for money."

What, we may ask, is the source of Alf's energy? What fuels his rage? I can only offer a guess but I sense it is the result of frustration, the result of his being a petty and powerless figure, locked into a "dead- end" job with no sense of the future. It is a consequence of stasis: there is no tomorrow for Alf in the sense that tomorrow will be no different from today. He is perfectly secure within the confines of his little world, which helps explain why he is so open and obvious. He is at the bottom of the totem pole and doesn't have to worry about offending anyone and losing "face."

And yet, underneath the rage, underneath the hate lavished on Wogs and the Labour Party and the whole intellectual elite of

liberal or radical persuasion, there is a diffuse sense of terror
in old Alf. He is stuck in is own Hell (which, as Sartre said, is
"other people") and he cannot justify his life, or English
politics, except by finding scapegoats, sacrificial victims who
have invaded the paradise that was England and prevented the
policies of the Conservative Party from working.(The tragedy
of the working people in America is that too many of them
hate and not enough of them vote. Alf, at least, I suspect is not
caught in that bind.)

Alan Goren of The Times has recognized this static quality in
the show and criticized it:

> Nothing happens. The great creation remains locked in
> his East End parlour, loggerheaded with his monster
> family, and waits for some news to break upon which his
> now familiar spleen can be predictably vented.

He concludes that "Alf has become a bore," and suggests that
Johnny Speight, who writes the show, "must make him do, not
just let him be." I would not agree, for the genius of the fool is
in being and not doing. The creation of contrived situations
would diminish and dilute Alf's personality.

Situation comedy rests on the triumph of situation over
individuality and personality; anyone, placed in certain
situations, becomes comic. A great character like Alf must be
comic and not be made comic.

The humor in the program is essentially verbal and is based on
insults, the revelation of ignorance, facetiousness, sarcasm,
and repartee. Dandy Nichols, who plays the wife (and who is a
much stronger figure than her American counterpart) is a
superb actress and is a perfect foil for Alf. She is a master of
the disdainful glance and the nasty repartee. In one program
which was based on a practical joke, the idea that his wife had
not made his evening meal, there was the following
conversation. Alf complained about not liking cheese
sandwiches.

Alf: "I'm not a bloody mouse!"
Wife: "I wish you were ... I'd set a trap for you."

There was also a scene in which Alf tried to get a word in
edgewise some six or eight times, but each time he said "Look
…" his wife interrupted him and rambled on.

The acting is generally quite superb and it helps to carry the
program. It also is very topical and manages to focus upon
some critical event in the political scene each week, as it rolls
along. Oil, the three-day week, etc. are all grist for its
militancy. We cannot be sure that the best lack all conviction,
but in Alf Garnett, we can have good reason to suspect that the
worst really are full of passionate intensity.

A REVELATION ABOUT ROYALTY

As an American I have always found the notion of real kings
and queens to be quite strange. When I was s. child I heard
countless fairy tales about kings and queens and assumed that
they were proper and suitable in the old days, but in modern
times? There is, of course, an egalitarian ethos in America that
makes us feel very uncomfortable about what we could call
"all this royalty nonsense." The idea that there are lords and
ladies, counts, barons, princes and princesses, dukes and
duchesses, etc. etc. is okay for the fairy tales, but not for real
life. We prefer our princes to be princes of commerce, men
who have achieved things on their own and not on the basis of

a. kind of "selective breeding."

There are many in England who feel the same way, though statistics show that the royal family is very popular, and the recent marriage of Princess Anne received elaborate media coverage and most of the English people felt very happy about the matter. The Republicans made great jest about the two partners, neither of whom seem particularly interesting or in any way remarkable. They share, it seems, a passion for horses and not very much else.

England now is a country which only maintains the illusion of power and a royal family is needed to help sustain the illusions. They are a very special kind of theatrical performers, who are kept busy with numerous social engagements and lend a kind of dignity to opening dams and underground stations, and that kind of thing. The Queen is rather matronly and sexless, but seems to be a decent enough person, though not remarkable in any way except one--she is the Queen.

Why, then, do the English keep a royal family? There are a number of reasons behind it. First, they have had kings and queens for a long time and anything that is traditional in England has considerable value, if only for pulling in the tourists. Pope said "whatever is, is right," and most of the English would agree with this, except that they might add whatever was also. (I am excluding social and political legislation from this discussion, though I should point out that they have been much more creative than Americans in some regards.)

Secondly, there seems to be a certain amount of sense in separating political power from moral and symbolic power. In America the President's family is the first family and the President is looked upon as a symbol of all that is great (and conversely, at times, evil) about America. Having a person who is a symbolic leader and not also the political leader is a good solution to this problem, though this can be done without a king or queen.

The real reason, I suspect, for having royalty is that it is possible, then, to print those wonderful "By Appointment" symbols on jars of jam or cans of green beans. These symbols confer great security and many other gratifications to the English public (as well as the Danish one and all others that have royal families). There is no problem of anxiety about what kind of ham to buy. For a. few pence more you get the kind the King of Denmark eats, and that should be good enough for anyone. The "By Appointment Symbols" are guarantees of propriety, and hopefully, of quality.

They also, in a subtle way, imply equality, since if we are what we eat, and we all eat items with "By Appointment" symbols on them, we are all the same, even if we don't all live in Buckingham Palace. Thus the Englishman is offered equality in the sphere of consumption and the royal family can be looked upon, in this regard, as idols of consumption. This points up a tangential. function of the royal family. They solidify and define lines of status, and remove doubts as to where one belongs (or what one eats when one wants "the best"). As a result of this you find a remarkable sense of assurance in English aristocratic families; they are "born to rule", and find support and confirmation in this, should they ever have a doubt, every time they reach for a jar of raspberry preserves.

The advertising industry plays up on the status conferred by these symbols and spurious imitations of them which "suggest" the "By Appointment Symbols" are found on many cigarette packages which seek to assure smokers that they are smoking quality cigarettes. What all of this proves is you don't have to be a king to live (almost) like one, though you may need a king's ransom!

BEER IN ENGLAND

Does "Malt do more than Milton can/ To justify the ways of God to man" in England? I'm not sure such is the case, but it does seem quite evident that beer plays an important part in the psyche (and social life) of the average Englishman. In this sense it is analogous to milk for the average American, for both confer psychic rewards and are intimately connected with the development of young people in the two countries.

Americans drink a great deal of beer but though, as the ads used to proclaim, "beer belongs" in America, it is not as important or central as in England. After the American has been weaned from milk there is a latency period and he begins with alcoholic beverages--beer and then hard liquor. The Englishman, on the other hand, tends to stay with beer and it is beer that is the "organizing" beverage around which the pub is constructed, and upon which much working class (and other) socializing revolves.

The public house, the public parlor--for people who have parlors or who have skimpy ones, is connected with certain basic myths about England: mateship, conviviality, maybe even courage (the name of a popular beer). And now that the saloon bar and public bar have merged, England is ready to proclaim itself, silently, that is, in its own imagination, on the verge of being a classless middle-class nation like America thinks it is.

Beer used to be, so everyone tells me, much better in the old days: it had body, it had character, it had strength. Now the traditional British malt beverages, bitter, brown ale and stout (which everyone tells me is "good for you and very nourishing") are under attack from thinner, lighter, more "refined" lagers. And as the beer gets thinner and less wholesome, the on-going party (which is what a pub is, especially for its locals) loses its centrality, and the myth of England, as a land of stout-filled stout hearted, stout drinking lads, fades. Conversation can't compete with the telly and canned beer is cheaper, anyway.

The pubs are not dead by any means, and when you go to one you are quite likely to find it buzzing, but it is not the center of the action in the social life of the working class now to the extent it was . Pubs are now getting more expensive, as television sets become cheaper. A recent article in one of the London newspapers said that many Englishmen will not be able to afford both cigarettes and beer and will have to choose one or the other.

In America people drink beer differently from the way they do in England, where the "pint" is the most common way of purchasing beer in a pub. In America it is frequently bought by the bottle, though many bars have draught beer and sell it in glasses or tankards. The Americans prefer lager and compared to English beer, most American beers are extremely light and somewhat more bitter. But Americans use bars differently, as a rule they are not as important to the social life of the ordinary working class American, who is much more home oriented (like his fellow middle class member of the bourgeoisie), and perhaps a bit more domesticated. And we don't produce the wide variety of malt beverages that the English do, though we do import beer and ale from everywhere; in part because we must.

In England beer is seen as connected with virility, power, strength and manhood. A recent ad for Double Diamond showed a man at the end of his first day off cigarettes, weakening as he inhaled fumes from other people who were smoking. Fortunately, he got a pint of Double Diamond and as he drank it, in an enormous and almost orgasmic swallow, his resolution firmed immediately. It made all the difference. If it was the playing fields of Eton that created the upper-class heroes who preserved democracy and provided leadership to the masses, it was the pubs of England that the bone-weary masses retreated: to repair their bodies and give their spirits a. lift, with beer that had body and character!

Those days have now passed; the English public schools are no longer full of people who are certain they were born to rule and the pubs are not full of people who can be led the nose and who can find solace only in strong beer. There is a theory which suggests that the working classes are becoming middle class and that this is a clever trick by the capitalists, who wish to "buy off" the masses by giving them a. stake in society. This theory of embourgeoisement might explain the inroads which lager has made in England.

The working classes, now with a petit-bourgeois mentality, have their stake (and kidney pie) in society and imitate the middle class types by drinking lighter beer and even hard liquor from time to time. Beer then does justify the ways of God and the ruling party to man in England. And there is little likelihood of a revolution as long as the working classes have the beers, their birds and their boob tubes. I would add that even without all the above there is little likelihood of revolution in England. A country of fish eaters, the English know their plaice.

(a sorry society)

SORRY!

One thing you have to realize about the English is that they don't mean "sorry" when they say "sorry" just as they don't mean "love" when they say "love." Sorry is just a noise they make, like love, in certain instances…when they've bumped into you in the supermarket, when they've. dialed the wrong number at 1.30 in the morning, when they've lost your money at the bank or hit you with a car. Then it comes, in the special way they have of saying it, with a faintly trilled "r" and slight emphasis on the last syllable. Sor-r-r-ee!

In addition to being a noise made in embarrassing situations, "sorry" is a statement about the way of the world, a kind of response to the universe, and a sorry one at that. Sorry means "too bad, but that's the way the cookie (crumpet) crumbles!" It is not a statement of personal regret. Sometimes "sorry" is extended to "sorry about that" which demonstrates this clearly. The person who says sorry is not saying "I regret" but rather "too bad, but nothing can be done!" There is a subtle kind of fatalism here, which can become amusing--when, for instance, two people bump into each other and both say "sorry." This statement in such cases is not apologetic but a philosophical pronouncement. What is more remarkable is that once uttered, the person is free to continue on doing the same thing over and over again, uttering "sorry" mechanically, as if saying "sorry" somehow justifies transgressions or errors. "Sorry" is a reductionist kind of confessional, similar to those made in the Catholic Church. You are purged of guilt and free to go out and sin all over again, but have you really admitted your guilt?

People don't say "I'm sorry," which would place responsibility on their shoulders. No, not indeed. "Sorry" is a statement that seems to suddenly appear, with no speaker behind it. Perhaps because it is heard so often, because there are so many "sorry's" floating about, we merely latch on to the one nearest, in point of time, to whatever mishap might have generated one?

On the other hand there is an element of self-forgiveness about it, as I mentioned earlier. If you don't want to think of it as a sacred word, tied to the confessional, think of it as a magic one, which confers forgiveness automatically. The magic utterance that cleanses the soul.

In America people don't say "sorry". Instead they say things like "pardon me" or "excuse me". This is much different. 'Sorry is a solipsistic statement; a person, for some reason, exclaims that he or she is "sorry" and that is the end of the matter. When you say "pardon me" you are really making a request: "will you please pardon me or excuse me?" You are taking cognizance of another person and asking to be excused, for some mishap that generated your request. "Sorry", then, is arrogant and self-centered. It might be translated "I (claim I) am sorry," but it does not take anyone else into account. It is a noise that expresses, in the final analysis, that a person exists and gives the state of this person's mind at a given moment. It is the kind of an utterance one might expect from a people who once "ruled" the seas and was a great imperial power; it is not a sign of politeness at all. Do you find this analysis a bit far-fetched? Do you think I'm too hard on the English? Do you believe I'm making a mountain out of a molehill?

Sorry!

OF CABBAGES AND KINGS;
THE UNIVERSTIES OF SUSSEX AND CAMBRIDGE

This week I spent some time at two very different universities Sussex and Cambridge. I went to Sussex to deliver a lecture on comics and society and it was a thoroughly proletarian experience. when I arrived at Falmer, which is where Sussex is located, just on the outskirts of Brighton, I was met by my host, a young member of the American Studies faculty, who shepherded me about. He led me to the faculty cafeteria, where I had a lunch of oxtail soup, pickled herring, a few vegetables, some stout, and an apple tart.

I chose that meal because there seemed little else that was edible available, and I could not work up an appetite given the surroundings. Several younger members of the department joined us for lunch and we chatted about politics, the reputation of Sussex as an "advanced and avant garde" institution, and things like that.

At 2.15 I was led into a rather nice lecture hall, which rapidly (to my great pleasure) filled up with students. "You've really packed them in", my host said to me, as the students filled the seats and overflowed onto the stairs. I then gave my lecture on "social themes in the comics" and was quite well received.

One of the students said "Keep on, tell us as much as you know," when I indicated that I was thinking of drawing my remarks to a close so we would have more time for questions. I lectured until 3.30, after which there were a few questions and the students left. I was then escorted to the tea lounge where my host bought me a cup of tea. We then returned to his office, but because of lighting restrictions he would not turn on the lights. "I can only turn it on when students are here," he told me. After about ten minutes in the fading gloom of the afternoon he informed me, apologetically, that I would have to go, as he had some students coming for a tutorial. He pointed me in the direction of the railway station, telling various students he passed on the way to "go in and sit down, and I'll be there in a moment," and left me to my own devices.

It was raining out and unpleasant, so I did not look about the campus very much, but I did get a sense of the place from its architecture. The new redbrick universities are very conscious of their identities and take some pains with their architecture. Since Oxford and Cambridge have a monopoly on the past, the red bricks must, somehow, capture the future, and you find rampant modernism--with round buildings, dramatic buildings, progressive buildings, etc. dotting the landscape.

There is a matter-of-factness in Sussex, just as there was at East Anglia, though it reminded me of a prison or corrective institution rather than an educational one. Sussex isn't quite like East Anglia, though both have a desire for flair, for a place in the sun--at least the architectural journals.

My visit to Cambridge was unexpected. I have a friend who is at one of the colleges there and whom I hadn't seen for fifteen years. After a number of attempts to arrange a meeting by mail I picked up the phone one night and called him up. We made arrangements for me to visit him the next day, and so two days after my visit to Sussex I found myself being shown Milton's Mulberry Bush and other treasures at Cambridge. My friend, Gorley Putt, had an absolutely gorgeous suite of rooms, full of old and elegant furnishings, and the whole scene was as far removed from Sussex as could be imagined.

"We shall dine in hall," he informed me, and then told me a bit about the ritual of dining there and of being inscribed into the wine books. We spent the afternoon catching up on ourselves and talking about literature and politics and that kind of thing until six, when he excused himself for an hour to put in his office hours.

After he returned we went to dinner, where I sat at the high table (or is it head table) and chatted with various members of the faculty. I happened to be placed with my back to the students, which meant that I faced John Milton, Charles Darwin and several other Cambridge men who had made a name for themselves.

The table was exquisitely set. Our first course was some kind of creamed seafood dish, in a shell, and it was quite delicious. This was followed by roast squab and vegetables and a fine red wine. After dinner we adjourned to another room where the wine ceremony took place. The queen was toasted, I was toasted, and then a bottle of Port was passed about while we ate fruit and chatted. A number of the people there left after a while, but several of us remained until midnight, at which time we left and my host and I talked until 2.30 AM He had a small guest room which was set for me and I slept beautifully.

Shortly after I got up, my host informed me that he had sent for breakfast, and pointed to the courtyard where two kitchen boys were carrying large trays full of plates and things for us. They came in and set the trays out--a large plate of corn flakes, which came in a big plate covered with a metal container; bacon and eggs, toast and coffee. We ate on a beautiful and elegant table underneath an exquisite chandelier. The whole thing was like something out of a Hollywood fantasy about

England and what Cambridge must be like. Yes, it was like that; people wore academic gowns to dinner, prayers were made in Latin, of course, and the whole place was steeped in the past, in tradition, in refined elegance, in a quiet sense of superiority. I don't know how much attention students get at Sussex, but I was astounded at the amount of attention they get Cambridge.

Cambridge is, however, unwilling to give up the future to its younger and brasher counterparts. At my friend's college they have just built a new dormitory which is as "modern" and futuristic as anything at Sussex--in fact, it is much nicer than anything I saw at either East Anglia or Sussex. Cambridge wants to have the best of both worlds--the past (which it and Oxford can lay claim to) and the future. Cambridge, in its quiet way, wants everything. It is Imperial and Imperialistic, but I do not think it has the power it once had.

In America we tend to dismiss the upper classes as playboys and spoiled types, assuming that it is the middle classes (or perhaps even now the blue-collar working classes) who are full of effort, optimism and energy and who will take over the country. This is absurd. The life chances of the rich are infinitely better than the poor, and the children of the rich are, as a rule, well-educated and extremely capable. And, they have what is invaluable…very good connections.

Educational institutions are social ones, also, which frequently lay claim to great loyalties and affection on the part of their members. I don't know whether Cambridge gets certain types, who fit a mold, or shapes young men and women who are "inclined" in certain directions. But there can be no question that three years at Cambridge (or Sussex, for that matter) with the kind of affectionate and intense attention that is offered there, must have a very powerful effect.

You can contrast this with what is the case in America, where a university education is generally not as total and as powerful an experience. Large numbers of students, who are working and studying at the same time, fit their education into their lives; it is not their lives as much as it is in England.

SHERLOCK HOLMES
Consulting Detective

There is a kind of richness and amplitude to Cambridge that I admire; it is warm and reassuring, it has traditions to guide you, it has greatness floating about and has produced legions of brilliant people who have had distinguished careers, revolutionized our thinking, etc. It is so old and secure and sure of itself--perhaps even certain of itself--that it can, I feel, do things which newer institutions might shy away from. (Aristocrats don't have to worry about what people might say.) But will it?

The question in my mind is whether Cambridge is seizing its opportunities. My host there chided me, good naturedly, about being a "sociologist" (which I'm not) and remarked that, fortunately, people like me were few and far between at Cambridge. The place is full of Egyptologists and Classicists and other people doing obscure and perhaps (even more to the glory of the place) useless things. All of this is part of the myth they like to keep going in Cambridge; they will make no concessions to the present or even the future, as the myth goes, though they don't mean it at all. Chairs for Egyptologists but none for Pop Culturists! That would be too common. Let Sussex offer lectures on the comics and the significant trivia of the present day, let East Anglia hold a conference on popular culture. In the Garden of Eden that Cambridge represents, the serpent of sociology is not wanted.

But wait! As I wandered through the grounds of Christ's College I looked into one of the common rooms in a dormitory and there, brilliantly electric and not very traditional at all, sat a pinball machine. The Trojan wall has been breached! And Cambridge, so a wag told me, is on the verge of discovering the twentieth century.

STASIS IN THE ENGLISH PSYCHE:
STANDING FOR PARLIAMENT
AND LAYING BACK AND DOING IT FOR THE QUEEN

Why is it that in America a politician "runs" for office and in England a person "stands" for Parliament? Can such a simple difference as this point to anything of consequence as far as English culture is concerned? Can it be that the English vocabulary (which is but a reflection of the English culture-code) emphasizes stasis and other kinds of static responses to life, as contrasted to American activism an optimism? .

We know, from such fields as semantics and linguistics, that language reflects values and beliefs and also conditions our behavior, sometimes to a greater degree than we can possibly imagine. If this is granted then an examination of some common figure of speech may be of some consequence. There are other examples that might be mentioned. I have already discussed the motionless soldiers of the Queen's Guard one sees at Buckingham palace. Why should the ability to suppress motion and any signs of life be so highly esteemed? Perhaps because stasis is fundamental in the English psyche--or at least the psyche of those who can consider standing for Parliament or serving in the Queen's Guard.

What I have been discussing fits in neatly with the basic English pattern of ascription, as contrasted with the American pattern of achievement, as a means of rising in the world. In an egalitarian society you achieve greatness; in an aristocratic and elitist society greatness is, so to speak, frequently "thrust upon you." People are more or less' chosen, by others in positions of consequence, to succeed them. In America, on the other hand, people believe (and to a certain degree it is possible) that they can thrust themselves forward, by working hard, gaining an advanced education, etc. and rise far beyond the station in which they were born.

Is it not curious, then, that in England one takes a "lift" and America you take an elevator. Lift connotes, in a vague way, a passivity; you are, somehow, lifted up, in a high building, with little effort on your own part. An elevator, on the other hand, is active and direct. You rise in the; world, and are not lifted up by something. The whole emphasis on place is allied to what I've been discussing.

If America is a chaos of people chasing after a place in the sun, England is an orderly and nicely arranged queue of people waiting in line quietly for the sun to shine on them, when it gets around to it. Everyone knows his place here; we are back in the middle ages and each occupies his niche in the Great Chain of Being. It all works nicely (especially for those at the top) as long as everyone accepts the rules of the game.

Curiously enough, this passivity also manifests itself in the way the English talk about sex; or, at any event, the English upper middle and educated classes. There is much amused talk of "laying back and doing it for England." In such cases the English are mocking their image in the popular imagination of being cold and sexless and only engaging in intercourse to procreate. The upper class English are supposed to be much keener on horses than women, and sex is some kind of a "dirty little secret that is indulged in for procreation (not recreation) we are led to believe.

As the classic joke goes, after intercourse a French woman says to her husband, "that was marvelous, Pierre;" an American woman says, "do you want to go to the movies?" and an English woman says, "are you feeling better now, dear?" These jokes demonstrate the power of stereotypes and myths to shape expectation and are not to be dismissed lightly. There is a cohesive pattern to the static imagery in England — for the notions of ascription and passivity and coldness link together and provide a code of conduct that influences people (without their recognizing it) a great deal.

The aggression that is lurking in such jokes is turned against the people who tell them about themselves, leading to a kind of paralysis. This, in turn, reinforces the "dead" quality of people, so we have a process in which images of passivity and stasis lead to "deadness" which then makes the images and stereotypes seem to be true. I will conclude with a famous joke about sex and English women.

A young English girl is on holiday in a foreign land and is swimming on a deserted beach, occupied by one other person. She has an accident and drowns. The other person pulls her ashore, tries artificial respiration and when that fails goes racing off to find help. Meanwhile a young man comes walking on the beach, sees the girl and unaware that she is dead, has intercourse with her. While he is doing this the other person returns and sees what is going on. "My God," he says, "she's dead!" "Oh," says the surprised man, "I thought she was English!"

Note: Americans are citizens and Britons are subjects, which makes a big difference, also.

TIRED OF LONDON

"When you are tired of London," said the good doctor, "you are tired of life!" I don't know how many times I've heard that phrase; it is, by now, imbedded in my psyche. And, indeed, the very frequency with which you hear it tends to give it even more of a factuality, even more of a kind of certainty. It catches us in a bind. If we, for any one of a number of possible reasons, do grow tired of London, then we must, so it is ordained, be tired of life. Who will admit to this?

Why might one be tired of London? I, for one, am not. Or, if I am, I certainly won't admit it to myself. But my situation is unusual. I am a visitor here and am free to come and go in and out and chase around London as I please. I am seldom caught in rush hours in the underground.

My days are free and I can do what I wish. Still, like many others, I suffer from the noise and the traffic and the fumes from the oars. I am "victimized" by the congestion and the cost of living, though London is by far the cheapest of the capital cities I might have chosen to live in. For the ordinary person in England, London presents special problems; it is so expensive that there aren't enough bus drivers, teachers, or policemen.

They can't afford to live here and so London struggles on, trying to cope with staff shortages in any number of different areas. This means that bus services are frequently sketchy, that the trains in the underground don't run as often as they might and that some schools are on half session.

These afflictions, of course, are not peculiar to London. Every great city has problems and some, like New York, may have problems that are insoluble. (New York may, in fact, have to be abandoned!) Relative to many large cities, London is a marvel of efficiency and organization; it seems to be working, though not as well as it might. But nothing ever works as well as it might or should, so London cannot be faulted in this respect. The social animal, man, is not characterized by reason or efficiency.

What bothers me about Dr. Johnson's proverb is not that he is wrong about London or right about it. It is the implicit brainwashing that he subjects us to. The statement comes to us with the full weight of Dr. Johnson's massive authority. It is also very catchy, and has a structure that is immediately grasped:

> When you are tired of L..
> You are tired of L.....

Over the course of the years an assertion becomes a truth. We are dealing with an advertising slogan, really, that plays upon people's fears of being inadequate and incorrect, of having botched their life, somehow. Most proverbs have this quality of being directive, of taking upon themselves an aura of certitude that they have no right to claim.

They are ideological and probably play a very great part in the thinking of most people. They form the core of un-thought-about, uncritically accepted, assumptions people have. These proverbs are the philosophy of the common man, who is hypnotized by their rhetorical structure and "obvious" good sense.

After all, who does not know, and believe, that "Power corrupts and absolute power corrupts absolutely," (which is not what Lord Acton said). Who would not agree that "a stitch in times saves nine" or that "a bird in the hand is worth two in the bush." And when it comes to love and matters of the heart, don't we all believe that "absence makes the heart grow fender!" All of us, that is, except those who recall that "out of sight means out of mind."

Shortly after I arrived in London a friend came over for coffee one night. During the course of the conversation his wife said to mine "Well - have you fallen in love with London yet?" There is no question of whether one will or will not "fall in love with London." Only the amount of time necessary for this to happen is questionable. There are, I believe, good reasons for a person to fall "in love" with London, but I do not believe that it is inconceivable that a person should fail to do so. In the same light, it is possible, imagine, for a person to be tired of London and not tired of life.

And who knows, it might even be that a person can be tired of life and not tired of London?

ABOUT THE AUTHOR

Arthur Asa Berger is professor emeritus of Broadcast and Electronic Communication Arts at San Francisco State University, where he taught between 1965 and 2003. He has published more than 70 books and 130 articles in a variety of journals. His books have been translated into eight languages and he has visited fifty countries in the course of his travels and lectures.

Among his recent books are

WHAT OBJECTS MEAN
An Introduction to Material Culture
Second Edition
ARTHUR ASA BERGER

Media, Myth and Society (Palgrave Pivot),
The Objects of Affection: Semiotics and Consumer Culture
(Palgrave Macmillan),

*What Objects Mean: An Introduction to Material Culture 2ⁿᵈ
edition* (Left Coast Press),
 Dictionary of Advertising and Marketing Concepts (Left
Coast Press) and
Bali Tourism (Haworth).

www.ingramcontent.com/pod-product-compliance
Lightning Source LLC
Chambersburg PA
CBHW070540290526
45790CB00002B/576